GOVERNMENT PROCEDURES AND OPERATIONS

CORPORATE TAXES

REFORM ISSUES AND EVALUATION OF FEDERAL EXPENDITURES

GOVERNMENT PROCEDURES AND OPERATIONS

Additional books in this series can be found on Nova's website under the Series tab.

Additional e-books in this series can be found on Nova's website under the e-book tab.

GOVERNMENT PROCEDURES AND OPERATIONS

CORPORATE TAXES

REFORM ISSUES AND EVALUATION OF FEDERAL EXPENDITURES

BRIANNE NATHANSON
EDITOR

nova publishers
New York

Library of Congress Cataloging-in-Publication Data

ISBN: 978-1-63321-922-9

Published by Nova Science Publishers, Inc. † New York

Contents

PREFACE

Tax expenditures—special exemptions and exclusions, credits, deductions, deferrals, and preferential tax rates claimed by corporations, individuals, or both—support federal policy goals but result in revenue forgone by the federal government. Congress and the administration are reexamining tax expenditures used by corporations as part of corporate tax reform. This book describes trends in the number of corporate tax expenditures and estimated corporate revenue losses since 1986; describes the use of corporate tax expenditures in 2011; and compares the size of corporate tax expenditures to federal spending by budget function and, for tax expenditures used only by corporations, identifies spending programs with similar purposes. This book also uses GAO's tax expenditures evaluation guide to determine what is known about the deferral of income for controlled foreign corporations; deferred taxes for certain financial firms on income earned overseas; and the graduated corporate income tax rate.

Chapter 1 - Tax expenditures—special exemptions and exclusions, credits, deductions, deferrals, and preferential tax rates claimed by corporations, individuals, or both—support federal policy goals but result in revenue forgone by the federal government. Congress and the administration are reexamining tax expenditures used by corporations as part of corporate tax reform. GAO was asked to examine issues related to corporate tax expenditures. This report: (1) describes trends in the number of corporate tax expenditures and estimated corporate revenue losses since 1986; (2) describes the use of corporate tax expenditures in 2011; and (3) compares the size of corporate tax expenditures to federal spending by budget function and, for tax expenditures used only by corporations, identifies spending programs with similar purposes. To address these objectives, GAO analyzed Department of the Treasury estimates of tax expenditure revenue losses from 1986 to 2011 and Internal Revenue Service 2010 data and interviewed agency officials. GAO also reviewed the legislative history and relevant studies to determine the reported purpose of corporate-only tax expenditures, and searched federal program lists to identify federal spending programs that appear to share a reported specific purpose similar to corporate-only tax expenditures. The programs identified as related were not reviewed by the agencies responsible for the programs.

Chapter 2 - Congress and the administration are reexamining tax expenditures used by corporations as part of corporate tax reform. These tax expenditures— special exemptions and exclusions, credits, deductions, deferrals, and preferential tax rates—support federal policy goals, but result in revenue forgone by the federal government.

GAO was asked to examine issues related to certain tax expenditures. This report uses GAO's tax expenditures evaluation guide to determine what is known about: (1) the deferral of income for controlled foreign corporations; (2) deferred taxes for certain financial firms on income earned overseas; and (3) the graduated corporate income tax rate. GAO combined the two deferral provisions for evaluation purposes.

GAO's guide suggests using five questions to evaluate a tax expenditure: (1) what is its purpose and is the purpose being achieved; (2) does it meet the criteria for good tax policy; (3) how is it related to other federal programs; (4) what are its consequences for the federal budget; and (5) how is its evaluation being managed? To address these questions, GAO reviewed the legislative history and relevant academic and government studies, analyzed 2010 Internal Revenue Service (IRS) data, and interviewed agency officials and tax experts.

Chapter 3 - A debate is underway about how the United States should tax foreign-source, corporate income. Currently, the United States allows domestic corporations to defer tax on the earnings of their foreign subsidiaries and also gives credits for foreign taxes paid, while most other developed countries exempt the active earnings of their multinational corporations' foreign subsidiaries from domestic tax. The debate has focused on economic issues with little attention to tax administration. GAO was asked to describe for a group of study countries with exemption systems: (1) the rules for exempting foreign-source income, and (2) the compliance risk and taxpayer compliance burden, such as recordkeeping, of the rules. The study countries, selected to provide a range of exemption systems, are Australia, Canada, France, Germany, and the Netherlands. For these countries GAO reviewed documents; interviewed government officials, academic experts, and business representatives; and compared tax policies, compliance activities and taxpayer reporting requirements.

In: Corporate Taxes
Editor: Brianne Nathanson
ISBN: 978-1-63321-922-9

Chapter 1

CORPORATE TAX EXPENDITURES: INFORMATION ON ESTIMATED REVENUE LOSSES AND RELATED FEDERAL SPENDING PROGRAMS*

United States Government Accountability Office

WHY GAO DID THIS STUDY

Tax expenditures—special exemptions and exclusions, credits, deductions, deferrals, and preferential tax rates claimed by corporations, individuals, or both—support federal policy goals but result in revenue forgone by the federal government. Congress and the administration are reexamining tax expenditures used by corporations as part of corporate tax reform. GAO was asked to examine issues related to corporate tax expenditures. This report: (1) describes trends in the number of corporate tax expenditures and estimated corporate revenue losses since 1986; (2) describes the use of corporate tax expenditures in 2011; and (3) compares the size of corporate tax expenditures to federal spending by budget function and, for tax expenditures used only by corporations, identifies spending programs with similar purposes. To address these objectives, GAO analyzed Department of

* This is an edited, reformatted and augmented version of the Highlights of GAO-13-339, a report to congressional requesters, dated March 2013.

the Treasury estimates of tax expenditure revenue losses from 1986 to 2011 and Internal Revenue Service 2010 data and interviewed agency officials. GAO also reviewed the legislative history and relevant studies to determine the reported purpose of corporate-only tax expenditures, and searched federal program lists to identify federal spending programs that appear to share a reported specific purpose similar to corporate-only tax expenditures. The programs identified as related were not reviewed by the agencies responsible for the programs.

WHAT GAO RECOMMENDS

GAO made no recommendations in this report. Treasury provided technical comments that were incorporated, as appropriate; IRS had no comments.

WHAT GAO FOUND

Estimated tax revenue that the federal government forgoes resulting from corporate tax expenditures increased over the past few decades as did the total number of corporate tax expenditures. In 2011, the Department of the Treasury estimated 80 tax expenditures resulted in the government forgoing corporate tax revenue totaling more than $181 billion. Many of these tax expenditures are broadly available to both corporate and individual taxpayers. More than two- thirds or 56 of the 80 tax expenditures used by corporations in 2011 were also used by individual taxpayers, such as other types of businesses not organized as corporations. Modifying any of these 56 tax expenditures as part of broader corporate tax reform would likely affect both corporate and individual taxpayers to some degree.

Corporate tax expenditures span a majority of federal mission areas, but their relative size differs across budget functions. The 80 corporate tax expenditures had estimated revenue losses in 12 of the 18 budget functions in 2011. Of the $181 billion in estimated corporate tax revenue losses, 81 percent was concentrated in the international affairs and housing and commerce budget functions, exceeding federal outlays in those budget functions. The 24 tax expenditures used only by corporations in 2011 provide support intended to encourage certain activities, such as energy production, or provide support for certain entity types, such as credit unions. A corporate tax expenditure may have multiple purposes: one narrowly focused on a specific activity or entity as well as broader or additional purposes pursuing national priorities or other activities. For example, 7 of the 24 corporate-only tax expenditures are aimed at encouraging or supporting specific energy sources and technologies, and these tax expenditures may also have broader national purposes such as promoting domestic energy production and energy security. In examining their narrowly focused reported purposes, one-third of the 24 corporate-only tax expenditures appear to share a similar purpose with at least one federal spending program.

ABBREVIATIONS

CFDA	Catalog of Federal Domestic Assistance
CBO	Congressional Budget Office
CRS	Congressional Research Service
GDP	gross domestic product
GPRAMA	Government Performance and Results Act Modernization Act of 2010
IRS	Internal Revenue Service
SOI	Statistics of Income

March 18, 2013

The Honorable John Lewis
Ranking Member
Subcommittee on Oversight
Committee on Ways and Means
House of Representatives

The Honorable Lloyd Doggett
House of Representatives

Each year, the federal government makes a significant commitment to corporate income tax expenditures, which are reductions in the federal corporate income tax liability that result from special exemptions and exclusions from taxation, deductions, credits, deferrals of tax liability, or preferential tax rates. Estimated corporate revenue losses represent the amount of revenue the federal government forgoes as a result of corporate tax expenditures. Tax expenditures play a central role in a number of Congress's and the administration's proposals for corporate tax reform. Discussion regarding corporate tax reform has involved modifying or repealing certain tax expenditures as a way to broaden the corporate tax base and using the resulting revenue gains to offset reduced revenue from lowering the corporate income tax rate. However, there is little agreement on how much corporate tax rates should be reduced; which tax expenditures should be repealed or modified to offset such a rate cut; and what, if any, changes would be made to the individual income tax system to account for other types of business organizations and individual taxpayers that claim the same tax expenditures as corporations.

Corporate tax expenditures cover a wide range of federal policy goals and may have one or more purposes that are also pursued by federal spending programs. As we recently reported, reassessments of tax expenditures benefit from understanding whether there are related spending programs.[1]

You requested that we provide information describing corporate tax expenditures. Specifically, this report: (1) describes trends in the number of corporate tax expenditures and aggregate corporate revenue losses since 1986; (2) describes the use of corporate tax expenditures in 2011; and (3) compares the size of corporate tax expenditures to federal spending by budget function and, for tax expenditures used only by corporations, identifies spending programs with similar purposes.[2]

To identify how corporate tax expenditures have changed in terms of their numbers and aggregate revenue loss, we analyzed Department of the Treasury (Treasury) estimates for fiscal years 1986 through 2011. We aggregated estimated corporate and individual revenue losses and also identified the number of tax expenditures with only estimated corporate revenue losses, those with both corporate and individual revenue losses, and those with only individual revenue losses.[3]

To describe the use of corporate tax expenditures, including the number of taxpayers claiming corporate-only tax expenditures, we analyzed Treasury revenue loss estimates for 2011 for corporate and individual taxpayer groups.[4] We defined corporate tax expenditures as those that Treasury reported had estimated revenue losses for corporations in 2011; we describe any tax expenditures that Treasury estimated lost only corporate tax revenue in 2011 as corporate-only tax expenditures. We also obtained, where available, estimates from the Internal Revenue Service (IRS) Statistics of Income (SOI) 2010 corporate sample on the number of corporate taxpayers claiming certain tax expenditures. These were the most recent estimates available at the time of our work. Similarly, we obtained publicly available fiscal year 2010 data from IRS's Tax Exempt and Government Entities division on certain corporate tax expenditures. To assess the reliability of the data and estimates, we reviewed agency documentation, interviewed agency officials, and reviewed our prior reports that have used the data and estimates. While we determined that the Treasury and IRS data and estimates were sufficiently reliable for our purposes, the IRS SOI corporate sample may not provide a precise estimate of the number of taxpayers claiming a tax expenditure when the number of taxpayers is very small.[5]

To compare corporate tax expenditures to federal spending by budget function, we summed the estimated revenue losses of corporate tax expenditures and compared them to federal outlays by budget function for 2011. To identify spending programs with reported purposes similar to corporate-only tax expenditures in 2011, we first identified the reported purpose of those tax expenditures by reviewing their legislative histories, our prior work, as well as work by the Congressional Research Service (CRS) and the Congressional Budget Office (CBO) that discussed the tax expenditures. We reviewed these sources for any discussion on the intent or rationale of the tax expenditures. For this report, we identified a narrow reported purpose, specific to the type of entity or activity that the corporate-only tax expenditures support or target. In identifying the narrow reported purposes we were not trying to discern the legislative intent. The corporate-only tax expenditures may have broader or additional purposes beyond the narrow reported purposes we identified. We used the narrow reported purposes as they allowed us to identify the tax and nontax programs that appear to most closely support the activity or entity the corporate-only tax expenditures support. We then searched the 2012 *Catalog of Federal Domestic Assistance* (CFDA) to identify federal spending programs that appear to share a similar reported purpose based on the CFDA's program descriptions. Our list of nontax programs that appear to share a similar reported purpose has not been reviewed by the agencies responsible for them. We identified tax expenditures that appear to share a similar reported purpose by reviewing their descriptions in the fiscal year 2013 *Analytical Perspectives*, supplemented with the description in CRS's 2010 tax expenditures compendium, and Treasury and IRS reviewed our identification of related tax expenditures.[6] See appendix I for more information on our scope and methodology.

We conducted our work from October 2012 to March 2013 in accordance with all sections of GAO's Quality Assurance Framework that are relevant to our objectives. The framework requires that we plan and perform the engagement to obtain sufficient and appropriate evidence to meet our stated objectives and to discuss any limitations in our work. We believe that the information and data obtained, and the analysis conducted, provide a reasonable basis for any findings and conclusions in this product.

BACKGROUND

Corporate tax expenditures are special tax provisions that are exceptions to the normal structure of the corporate income tax system.[7] They represent revenue the federal government forgoes from these tax provisions. The Congressional Budget and Impoundment Control Act of 1974 identified six types of tax provisions that are considered tax expenditures when they are exceptions to the normal tax structure, including exemptions, exclusions, deductions, credits, deferral, and preferential tax rates.[8] Treasury and the Joint Committee on Taxation each compile an annual list of tax expenditures by budget function with estimates of the corporate and individual income tax revenue losses for each tax expenditure in their respective lists.[9] Treasury and the Joint Committee on Taxation calculate separately the estimated revenue losses for each tax expenditure under the assumptions that all other tax expenditures remain in the tax code and taxpayer behavior remains constant.[10] Thus, the estimated revenue losses do not represent the amount of revenue that would be gained if a particular tax expenditure was repealed, since repeal would probably change taxpayer behavior in some way that would affect revenue.

Corporate income tax expenditures are estimated for firms organized under the tax code as C corporations, which include most large, publicly held corporations, and have their profits taxed at the entity level under the corporate income tax system (filed on an IRS form 1120). Other types of businesses, such as partnerships and S corporations[11], are referred to as "pass-through" entities because for tax purposes the income earned by these businesses is attributed to or passed through to the owners of the business and are in general taxed only once under the individual income tax system. Treasury and the Joint Committee on Taxation classify the estimated amounts of tax expenditures claimed (or used) by "pass- through" entities as individual income tax expenditures.[12]

The classification of a tax expenditure as corporate or individual, or both is based on the entity that claims or uses the particular tax provision or would report a type of income if it were not excluded from tax. This classification reflects what is referred to as the statutory incidence of the tax expenditure and shows which entities—corporations or individuals, or both—can directly reduce their tax liability because of the tax expenditure. However, as both Treasury and the Joint Committee on Taxation note, the benefits and outcomes from the tax expenditure may be intended to ultimately benefit people other than the direct recipients of the tax expenditure. To the extent that a tax expenditure leads to changes in the prices of particular goods or services, wages, or returns on investment, consumers, employees, or shareholders may see benefits that they otherwise would not have received. A classification based on ultimate beneficiaries would reflect what is known about the economic incidence of tax expenditures rather than the statutory incidence.[13] For example, the credit for low-income housing investments, while claimed largely by corporate taxpayers, is intended to ultimately benefit individuals by stimulating the production of affordable rental housing and thereby enabling low-income households to obtain potentially higher quality housing for lower rent than they would have otherwise.

Over the past decade, the number of corporate taxpayers has declined, partly because more businesses are organizing as "pass-through" entities than as C corporations. In tax year 2010, IRS reported that almost 1.7 million active C corporations filed an IRS form 1120, down from 1.9 million in tax year 2007 and 2.2 million in tax year 2000.[14] Measured relative to the economy as a share of gross domestic product (GDP), corporate income tax receipts increased in the years leading up to the economic recession that began in December 2007. During this period they increased from 2.1 percent of GDP in 2000 to 2.7 percent of GDP in 2007 and have since decreased to 1.2 percent of GDP in 2011.[15]

Both members of Congress and the administration have outlined potential frameworks and proposals for modifying and simplifying the corporate income tax system in recent years. A number of these proposals have involved modifying or repealing some corporate tax expenditures to broaden the corporate income tax base and using the resulting revenue offset to reduce corporate income tax rates. One notable challenge for broader corporate tax reform is the degree to which changes to tax expenditures affect other types of taxpayers claiming them as most corporate tax expenditures are also available to other types of business entities other than corporations.

In selecting activities to fund federal policy goals, Congress can choose to enact a tax expenditure rather than a spending program or vice versa for a variety of reasons. We have developed and highlighted criteria and questions for evaluating tax expenditures, including whether other policy tools, such as spending programs, are preferable to tax expenditures.[16] In addition, we have long reported that, once enacted, tax expenditures and their relative contributions toward achieving federal missions and goals are often less visible than spending programs, which are subject to a more systematic review of performance, including results.[17] More recently, the Government Performance and Results Act (GPRA) Modernization Act of 2010 (GPRAMA)[18] established a framework for providing a more crosscutting and integrated approach to focusing on results and improving government performance, including for tax expenditures. GPRAMA makes clear that the Office of Management and Budget, in coordination with federal agencies, is to identify, among other things, the various federal agencies, program activities, and tax expenditures that contribute to the federal government's performance plan that defines the level of performance to be achieved toward crosscutting priority goals. These crosscutting priority goals cover a limited number of policy areas as well as goals to improve management across the federal government. Moving forward, GPRAMA implementation can help inform tough choices in setting priorities as policymakers address the rapidly building fiscal pressures facing our national government.[19]

ESTIMATED REVENUE LOSSES FROM CORPORATE TAX EXPENDITURES AND THE NUMBER OF CORPORATE TAX EXPENDITURES HAVE INCREASED SINCE 1986

Estimated revenue losses from corporate tax expenditures have increased over the last few decades in constant dollars, as shown in figure 1. After decreasing in the years following the Tax Reform Act of 1986, due to changes to both tax rates and tax expenditures, corporate revenue losses increased thereafter. Individual revenue losses also increased, although at a faster pace than corporate revenue losses.

From 1986 through 2011, the number of tax expenditures with estimated corporate revenue losses increased from 61 in 1986 to 80 in 2011, as shown in figure 2.[20]

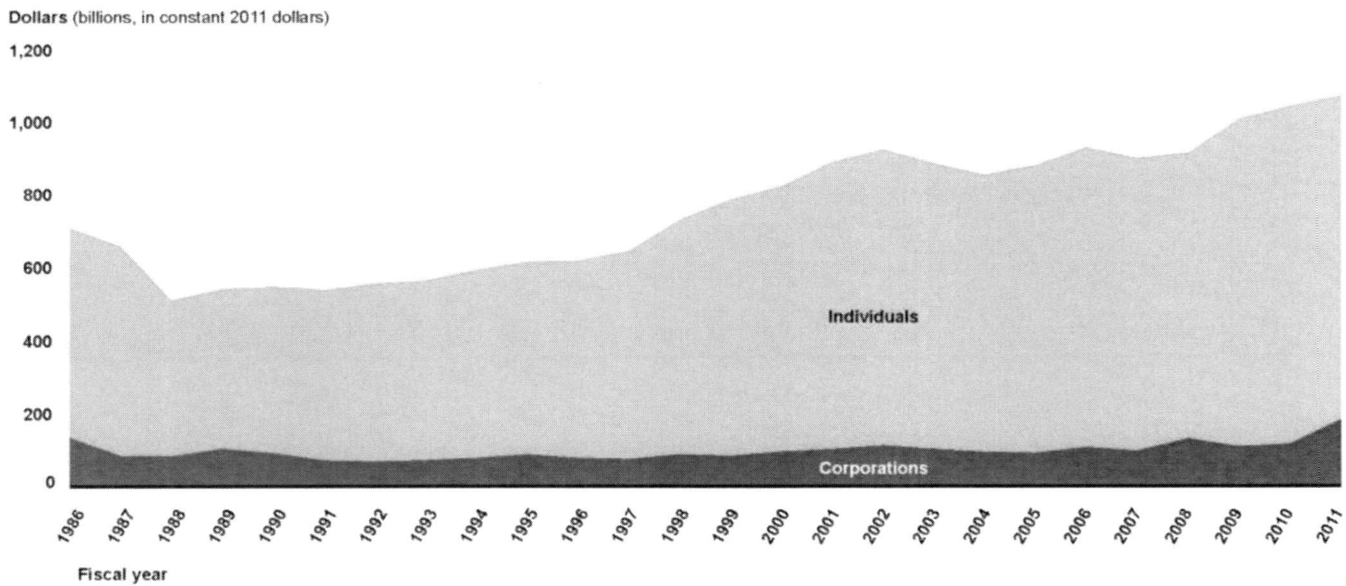

Source: GAO analysis of Office of Management and Budget reports, fiscal years 1988-2013.
Note: Sum of estimated revenue losses does not include outlay effects or reductions in excise tax receipts.

Figure 1. Comparison of Estimated Federal Tax Revenue Loss Due to Tax Expenditures for Corporations and Individuals Reported by Treasury, 1986 through 2011.

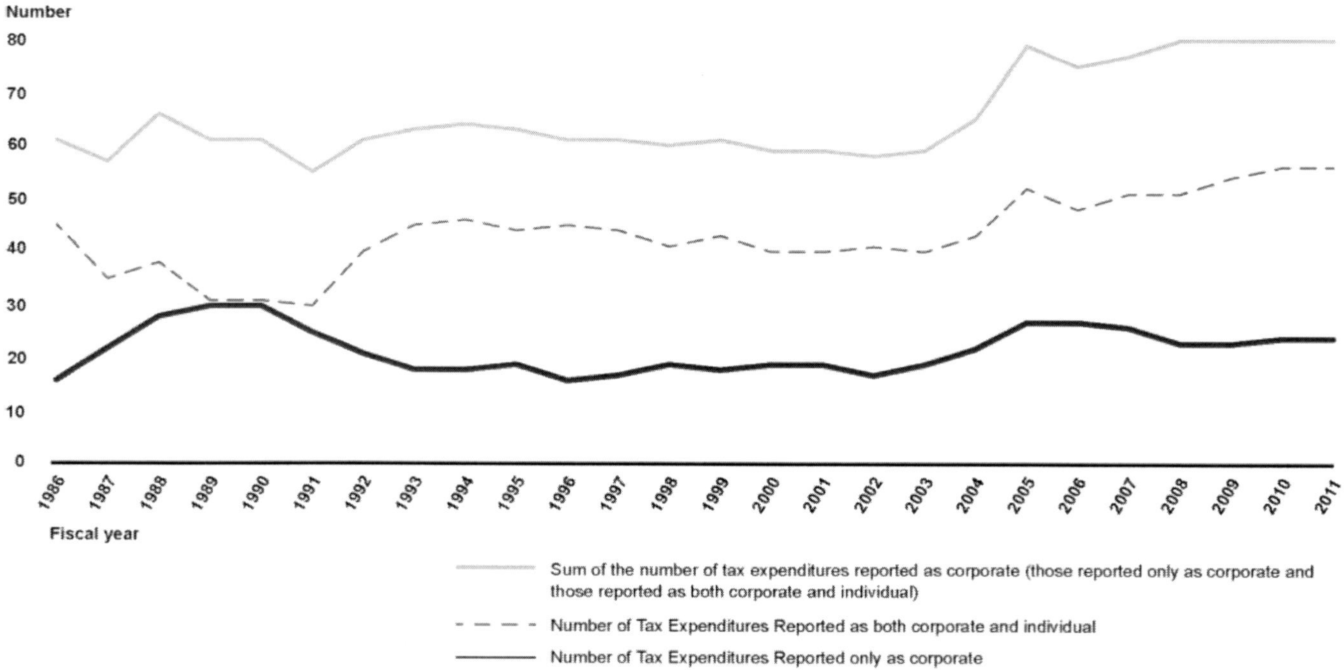

Source: GAO analysis of Office of Management and Budget reports, fiscal years 1988-2013.

Note: Tax expenditures may be available to corporate and individual taxpayers, including other types of business entities other than corporations. According to Treasury's estimates, some tax expenditures may be used by only corporate taxpayers and some by only individual taxpayers while other tax expenditures may be used by both corporate and individual taxpayers.

Figure 2. Number of Corporate Tax Expenditures Reported by Treasury, 1986 through 2011.

More Than Two-Thirds of Corporate Tax Expenditures Are Also Used by Individuals

Estimated corporate revenue losses in 2011, which totaled $181.4 billion, were approximately the same size as the amount of corporate income tax revenue the federal government collected that year. Individual tax revenue losses totaled $891 billion in 2011, and included tax expenditures used by other types of business entities that pass through to individual taxpayers. According to Treasury's 2011 estimates, 80 tax expenditures had corporate revenue losses. Of those, two expenditures accounted for 65 percent of all estimated corporate revenues losses in 2011 while another five tax expenditures—each with at least $5 billion or more in estimated revenue loss for 2011—accounted for an additional 21 percent of corporate revenue loss estimates. Table 1 shows the seven largest corporate tax expenditures in 2011.

A majority of corporate tax expenditures are not isolated to the corporate income tax system but also apply to other types of businesses, including "pass-through" entities. Of the 80 tax expenditures used by corporations, 56 were also used by individuals, as shown in figure 3. Modifying any of these 56 tax expenditures as part of broader corporate tax reform would likely affect both corporate and individual taxpayers to some degree. However, the percentage of corporate taxpayers using these tax expenditures varies considerably across the 56 tax expenditures. For example, some tax expenditures are predominately used by corporations, such as the alcohol fuels credit, with estimated corporate revenue losses comprising 96 percent of the tax expenditure's estimated $500 million income tax revenue loss in 2011.[21] Others are used predominantly by individuals, such as the exclusion of utility conservation subsidies, where corporations account for less than 5 percent of the $220 million estimated revenue loss in 2011. See appendix II for more information on these 56 tax expenditures' estimated corporate revenue losses in 2011.

The remaining 24 tax expenditures had only estimated corporate revenue losses in 2011. Some tax expenditures are limited to C corporations based on requirements in the Internal Revenue Code, which is why they have only corporate revenue losses, while others may not be restricted to C corporations but are only used by corporations in practice.[22] Modifying only those tax expenditures used by corporations as part of corporate tax reform may limit the changes to tax expenditures claimed only by corporate taxpayers but would limit somewhat the degree to which the corporate tax base could be broadened to pay for a corporate tax rate cut. See appendix III for a list of corporate-only tax expenditures. The number of corporations claiming a particular corporate-only tax expenditure varies. For example, in 2010 almost 12,000 organizations claimed the tax exemption for certain insurance companies owned by tax-exempt organizations ($200 million in corporate tax revenue losses in 2011) while 5 corporations claimed the credit for energy efficient appliances ($280 million in corporate tax revenue losses in 2011).[23] See appendix IV for the numbers of users for 11 corporate-only tax expenditures where data were available.

Table 1. Seven Largest Corporate Tax Expenditures, 2011

Tax expenditure	Federal revenue loss estimates resulting from corporations (dollars in billions)	Share of total estimated corporate tax revenue losses
Accelerated depreciation of machinery and equipment[a]	$76.1	42%
Deferral of income from controlled foreign corporations	41.4	23
Deduction for US production activities[b]	9.8	5
Credit for increasing research activities[c]	8.3	5
Exclusion of interest on public purpose State and local bonds[d]	7.6	4
Deferred taxes for financial firms on certain income earned overseas	6.2	3
Credit for low-income housing investments[e]	5.8	3
Total	**$155.3**	**86%**

Source: GAO analysis of Office of Management and Budget budget data on tax expenditures, fiscal year 2013.

Note: Totals may not add due to rounding.

[a] Also had estimated individual revenue losses of $42.4 billion in 2011.

[b] Also had estimated individual revenue losses of about $3.3 billion in 2011.

[c] Also had estimated individual revenue losses of $460 million in 2011.

[d] Also had estimated individual revenue losses of about $18.6 billion in 2011.

[e] Also had estimated individual revenue losses of $310 million in 2011. In addition, the credit for low- income housing investments has outlay effects of nearly $3.5 billion in 2011.

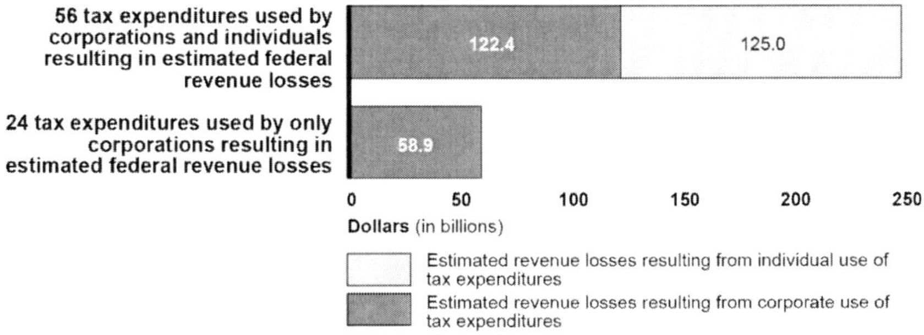

Source: GAO analysis of Office of Management and Budget data on tax expenditures, fiscal years 2013.

Note: Sum of estimated revenue losses does not include outlay effects or reductions in excise tax receipts. Tax expenditures may be available to corporate and individual taxpayers, including other types of business entities other than corporations. According to Treasury's estimates, some tax expenditures may be used by only corporate taxpayers and some by only individual taxpayers while other tax expenditures may be used by both corporate and individual taxpayers.

Figure 3. Estimated Federal Tax Revenue Losses Resulting from Corporate Tax Expenditures, 2011.

Corporate Tax Expenditures Span Many Budget Functions; One-Third of Corporate-Only Tax Expenditures Share a Similar Purpose with Federal Spending Programs

Corporate Tax Expenditures Span Many Budget Functions, and Estimated Corporate Revenue Losses Are Concentrated in Two Budget Functions

Corporate tax expenditures span a majority of federal mission areas, but their relative size differs across budget functions. The 80 corporate tax expenditures had estimated revenue losses in 12 of the 18 budget functions in 2011, as shown in table 2. Of the $181 billion in estimated corporate tax revenue losses, 81 percent was concentrated in the international affairs and housing and commerce budget functions. In these two budget functions, estimated corporate revenue losses were more than federal outlays.

Table 2. Numbers and Estimated Federal Revenue Losses Resulting from Corporate Tax Expenditures by Budget Function, 2011

Budget function	Number of corporate tax expenditures	Estimated corporate tax revenue losses (dollars in billions)[a]	Federal outlays (dollars inbillions)
Commerce and housing	16	$96.3	$(12.6)[b]
International affairs	3	50.8	45.7
General science, space, and technology	2	9.3	29.5
General purpose fiscal assistance	1	7.6	7.5
Energy	20	6.1	12.2
Education, training, employment, and social services	10	4.0	101.2
Health	5	2.8	372.5
Community and regional development	8	1.8	23.8
Natural resources and environment	8	1.5	45.5
Income security	1	1.0	597.4
Transportation	3	0.2	93.0
Agriculture	3	0.04	20.7
Total	**80**	**$181.4**[c]	**$1,336.2**

Source: GAO analysis of Office of Management and Budget budget data on tax expenditures and federal outlays, fiscal year 2013.

Notes: Budget functions are sorted by estimated corporate revenue losses. The national defense, social security, veterans benefits and services, and net interest budget functions had no corporate tax expenditures. While Treasury classifies each of the tax expenditures it lists under a particular budget function, some tax expenditures, such as those in the commerce and housing budget function may be claimed by various industries and potentially cut across multiple budget functions.

[a] The sum of estimated revenue losses does not include outlay effects or reductions in excise tax receipts. Outlay-equivalent estimates—the amount of outlays required to deliver the same after-tax income as provided through the tax expenditure—may provide for a more appropriate comparison to federal spending than estimated revenue losses if particular outlays represent taxable income to the recipient. However, Treasury no longer estimates outlay equivalent values for tax expenditures and therefore estimated revenue losses were used instead.

[b] The outlays are negative for this budget function as the present value of expected government collections for loan guarantee programs exceeds the present value of expected payments over the course of the loan guarantee in this particular year.

[c] Fifty six of the 80 corporate tax expenditures also had individual revenue losses from individual taxpayers and other business entities using these tax expenditures totaling $125 billion in 2011.

Corporate-Only Tax Expenditures Support Certain Activities or Entities and May Seek to Contribute to Broader National Results

Corporate-only tax expenditures generally support or encourage a specific type of entity or activity. See appendix V for the reported purposes for the 24 corporate-only tax expenditures that were the basis for our identification of related federal activities. Some of these tax expenditures have multiple reported purposes that are broader and in pursuit of national priorities. For example, seven corporate-only tax expenditures are aimed at encouraging or supporting the production of specific energy sources or the development of technology or infrastructure for certain energy sectors. These tax expenditures also have broader purposes such as promoting domestic energy production and energy security.

Other corporate-only tax expenditures provide support for certain types of entities, such as insurance companies or credit unions. Beyond providing support for these entities, these corporate-only tax expenditures may have additional purposes, which are different or broader in scope, related to why these types of entities receive tax support. However some of these tax expenditures were granted to entities prior to World War II and the rationale for continuing support to these entities may have changed over time, making it difficult to determine the purpose of providing the support. Our previous work highlighted the changing historical basis for one of these tax expenditures—the tax exemption of credit union income—as shown in figure 4.

One-Third of the Tax Expenditures Used Only by Corporations Appear to Share a Similar Purpose with Federal Spending Programs

Of the 24 corporate-only tax expenditures, one-third appear to share a similar purpose with federal spending programs. The largest number of these tax expenditures support purposes related to energy- and natural resources and environment-related purposes. These tax expenditures can be broken into two groups: (1) those aimed at encouraging fossil fuel production and development, and (2) those that are intended to encourage technology development, renewable energy, or energy efficiency. We identified related spending programs that appear to share a similar reported purpose with tax expenditures for the second category, but none for the first. See appendix VI for a summary list of related federal spending programs and activities.

While we identified related federal spending programs based on reported purposes specific to the entity or activity being supported, a number of these tax expenditures may also have one or more reported purposes that pursue broader or different aims. If a broader reported purpose was used, the extent of related spending programs identified may change considerably. For example, the bio-diesel and small agri-biodiesel producer tax credits, one of the corporate-only tax expenditures in 2011, have a specific reported purpose of encouraging production of biodiesel fuels, and we identified three federal spending programs that appear to share a similar purpose. Using a broader purpose for this tax expenditure would likely increase the number of federal spending programs identified that have a similar purpose. For example, our prior work on renewable energy identified nearly 700 federal initiatives related to renewable energy, including the bio-diesel and small agri-biodiesel producer tax credits.[24] Applying an even broader national purpose, such as encouraging domestic energy production, could further increase the number of federal spending programs, as well as other federal activities, such as federal regulations and tax expenditures, which may share a similar purpose. Alternatively, applying a different purpose, such as supporting rural and farm areas, could lead to identifying different federal programs that may share a similar purpose.

Unlike other depository institutions, credit unions are exempt from federal corporate income taxes. Congress originally granted tax-exempt status to credit unions in 1937 because of their similarity to other mutually owned financial institutions that were tax-exempt at that time. While the other institutions lost their exemption in the Revenue Act of 1951, credit unions specifically remained exempted. The act's legislative history is silent regarding why the tax-exempt status of credit unions was not revoked. More recently, the Credit Union Membership Access Act of 1998 indicates that credit unions continue to be exempt because of their cooperative, not-for-profit structure, which is distinct from other depository institutions, and because credit unions historically have emphasized serving people of modest means.

Source: GAO, Financial Institutions: Issues Regarding the Tax-Exempt status of Credit Unions, GAO-06-220T (Washington, D. C.: Nov. 3, 2005).

Figure 4. Historical Basis for the Tax Exemption of Credit Union Income.

Agency Comments and Our Evaluation

We provided a draft of this report to the Secretary of the Treasury and the Acting Commissioner of Internal Revenue for comment. Treasury provided technical comments which we incorporated; IRS had no comments on the report.

James R. White
Director, Tax Issues
Strategic Issues

Appendix I. Objectives, Scope, and Methodology

This report: (1) describes trends in the number of corporate tax expenditures and aggregate corporate revenue losses since 1986; (2) describes the use of corporate tax expenditures in 2011; and (3) compares the size of corporate tax expenditures to federal spending by budget function and, for tax expenditures used only by corporations, identifies spending programs with similar purposes.

Trend Analysis of Treasury Tax Expenditure Estimates

To identify how corporate tax expenditures have changed in terms of their numbers and aggregate estimated revenue losses, we analyzed tax expenditure estimates developed by the Department of the Treasury (Treasury) and reported by the Office of Management and Budget in the Federal Budget's *Analytical Perspectives* for fiscal years 1986 through 2011. For this period, we determined which tax expenditures had estimates only for corporations, for both corporations and individuals, and only for individuals.[25] We then summed the estimated revenue losses and the number of tax expenditures by taxpayer group to determine changes over time in trend data and to see how the amounts differed between these taxpayer groups.[26] We converted all sums for each fiscal year into 2011 constant dollars to adjust for inflation using the chain price indexes reported in the fiscal year 2013 federal budget. While sufficiently reliable as a gauge of general magnitude, summing revenue loss estimates does not take into account any interactions between tax expenditures. In addition, revenue loss estimates do not incorporate any behavioral responses and, thus, do not represent the revenue amount that would be gained if a specific tax expenditure was repealed.[27]

Fiscal Year 2011 Analysis of Treasury Tax Expenditure Estimates and Internal Revenue Service Data on Number of Recipients

For 2011, we analyzed those tax expenditures with only estimated corporate revenue losses and those with both corporate and individual revenue losses.[28] For this study, we defined corporate tax expenditures as those that Treasury reported had estimated revenue losses for corporations in 2011; we describe any tax expenditures that Treasury estimated lost only corporate tax revenue as corporate-only tax expenditures. We did not conduct a legal analysis to determine which tax expenditures are available only to corporations.

To describe the number of taxpayers claiming corporate-only tax expenditures, we obtained estimates, where available, from the Internal Revenue Service (IRS) Statistics of Income (SOI) 2010 corporate sample on the number of corporate taxpayers claiming each of the corporate-only tax expenditures. These were the most recent estimates available at the time of our work. Data compiled by IRS SOI is based on a stratified, random sample of 63,630 corporate income tax returns for 2010 from corporations that end their corporate year from July 1, 2010, through June 30, 2011. These estimates are subject to sampling errors. Based on the number of sampled returns and the coefficients of variation provided by SOI, we estimate that the upper bound of a 95 percent confidence interval for the estimated total number is less than 830 corporations for the following tax expenditures: alternative fuel production credit, bio-diesel and small agri-biodiesel producer tax credits, credit for energy efficient appliances, employer-provided child care credit, tax credit for orphan drug research, small life insurance company deduction, and Special Blue Cross/Blue Shield deduction. For our report, IRS SOI provided data on C corporations, and we excluded S corporations that pass through to individual taxpayers. C corporations include active corporations filing tax forms 1120, 1120-F, 1120-L, and 1120-PC but not tax forms 1120S, 1120-REIT, and 1120-RIC. Overall, IRS SOI was able to provide estimates for nine tax credits or deductions because these tax expenditures were reported on an isolated line of an IRS form. However, for two of those tax credits, the requirement to protect taxpayer information forced IRS to exclude estimates of the number of tax recipients of those credits.[29]

We also obtained publicly available fiscal year 2010 data from IRS's Tax Exempt and Government Entities division on four corporate-only tax expenditures. These corporate-only tax expenditures were tax exemptions and included the exemption of credit union income, tax exemption of certain insurance companies owned by tax-exempt organizations, exemption of certain mutuals' and cooperatives' income, and special alternative tax on small property and casualty insurance companies. For three of the four tax expenditures that we obtained publicly available data on the number of organizations claiming the tax exemption, the data represented only a portion of organizations to which the exemption applies as reporting requirements differ within each of these tax expenditures. From these two sources, IRS SOI estimates and publicly available data from IRS's Tax Exempt and Government Entities division, we were able to obtain data on the number of taxpayers claiming 13 of the 24 corporate-only tax expenditures, including credits, deductions, or exemptions. IRS was not able to provide data on the remaining eleven tax expenditures generally because they could not be isolated on an IRS form. To assess the reliability of the data and estimates, we reviewed agency documentation, interviewed agency officials, and reviewed our prior reports that have used the data and estimates. While we determined that the Treasury and IRS data and estimates were sufficiently reliable for our purposes, the IRS SOI corporate sample may not provide a precise estimate of the number of taxpayers claiming a tax expenditure when the number of taxpayers is very small.[30]

Comparison of Estimated Revenue Losses and Federal Outlays and Reported Purpose and Those Federal Activities That Appear to Share a Similar Purpose

To analyze how large corporate tax expenditures are in comparison to federal spending by budget function, we summed the estimated revenue losses for those tax expenditures with corporate revenue losses in fiscal year 2011 by budget function from the fiscal year 2013 *Analytical Perspectives*. We compared them to federal outlays by budget function in fiscal year 2011, using data from the President's fiscal year 2013 budget. Outlay-equivalent estimates—the amount of outlays required to deliver the same after-tax income as provided through the tax expenditure—may provide for a more appropriate comparison to federal spending than estimated revenue losses if particular outlays represent taxable income to the recipient. However, Treasury no longer estimates outlay equivalent values for tax expenditures and therefore, estimated revenue losses were used instead.

For this report we identified related programs based on a narrow reported purpose specific to the type of entity or activity that the corporate-only tax expenditures support or target. The corporate-only tax expenditures may have additional broader or different purposes. Using the narrow reported purposes allowed us to identify the tax and nontax programs that appear to most closely support the activity or entity the corporate-only tax expenditures support. We defined the narrow reported purpose as providing support for a certain activity or entity or in some cases, where the materials we reviewed discussed the tax expenditure as intended to encourage or increase a certain activity, we described the reported purpose as encouraging that type of activity. To identify the reported purpose of corporate-only tax expenditures, we reviewed their legislative histories and prior work by GAO, the Congressional Research Service (CRS), including the CRS's 2010 tax expenditure compendium, and the Congressional Budget Office (CBO) that discussed the intended purpose or rationale of the tax expenditure.[31] However, in identifying the narrow reported purposes we were not trying to discern legislative intent. For some tax expenditures, the reported purpose may be clear from reviewing these sources, while for others the reported purpose may be more difficult to determine. Some tax expenditures support a certain type of entity but the reported purpose or rationale for providing support to that entity is difficult to determine or may have changed over time. Therefore, we describe the reported purpose as support for a type of entity, and we did not reconstruct the historical basis for providing such support.[32]

To identify federal spending programs that appear to share a similar reported purpose, we searched the October 2012 version of the *Catalog of Federal Domestic Assistance* (CFDA) using terms from the description of the corporate-only tax expenditures. We reviewed programs listed under the same budget functions and reviewed the descriptions of the programs initially identified to determine if they appear to share a similar reported purpose. We identified related tax expenditures by reviewing the fiscal year 2013 *Analytical Perspectives*, supplemented with the description in CRS's 2010 tax expenditure compendium.[33]

For the inventory of related federal spending programs and tax expenditures, we collected descriptive information about each program, including (1) the name of the program, (2) the administering or implementing agencies or entities, and (3) the type of assistance provided. This information was collected from the October 2012 CFDA, fiscal year 2013 *Analytical Perspectives*, and agency documentation.[34] The data we collected from the October 2012 CFDA for each of these three data elements was entered in the CFDA by the federal agencies responsible for the programs, but the agencies responsible did not verify our analysis of those data or identification of related programs. After reviewing CFDA documentation, our prior reports that have used the data, and spot checking these three data element against other publicly available agency documentation, we determined the data were reliable for our purposes. In reporting the administering or implementing agencies or entities, we generally reported the federal department level rather than the sub-department level agency except for IRS and the Environmental Protection Agency. In addition, for reporting the type of assistance, we grouped the types of assistance into the following categories: grant, cooperative agreement, direct payment, direct loan, guaranteed loan, insured loan, regulation/standard, tax exclusions, exemptions, or deductions, tax credits, deferrals of tax, and preferential tax rates. In some cases, the CFDA identified the programs we identified as providing multiple types of assistance listed above.

The list of nontax programs we identified that appear to share a similar specific reported purpose has not been reviewed by the agencies responsible for them. Treasury and IRS reviewed our identification of related tax expenditures. The list of tax and nontax programs, shown in appendix VI, does not represent a comprehensive list of related federal activities for several reasons:

- The CFDA may not capture certain types of federal activities, such as regulations or standards. Based on our prior work, we were able to identify some regulatory programs which we believe also appear to share a similar reported purpose to the tax expenditures in our scope.
- The federal spending programs and activities identified may also have multiple reported purposes, and only a component of the program or activity may appear to specifically share a similar reported purpose to the tax expenditure.
- Using a broader or different reported purpose to identify federal activities that appear to share a similar reported purpose would likely alter the makeup of activities that appear to be related.

We conducted our work from October 2012 to March 2013 in accordance with all sections of GAO's Quality Assurance Framework that are relevant to our objectives. The framework requires that we plan and perform the engagement to obtain sufficient and appropriate evidence to meet our stated objectives and to discuss any limitations in our work. We believe that the information and data obtained, and the analysis conducted, provide a reasonable basis for any findings and conclusions in this product.

APPENDIX II. FIFTY-SIX TAX EXPENDITURES WITH ESTIMATED CORPORATE AND INDIVIDUAL REVENUE LOSSES REPORTED BY TREASURY, BY LARGEST ESTIMATED CORPORATE REVENUE LOSSES, 2011

Tax expenditure	Estimated corporate revenue losses (dollars in millions)	Corporate share of total estimated revenue losses[a]	Budget function
Accelerated depreciation of machinery and equipment	$76,140	64.2%	Commerce and housing
Deduction for U.S. production activities	9,840	74.9	Commerce and housing
Credit for increasing research activities	8,300	94.7	General science, space, and technology
Exclusion of interest on public purpose State and local bonds	7,570	28.9	General purpose fiscal assistance
Credit for low-income housing investments[b]	5,840	95.0	Commerce and housing
Exclusion of interest on life insurance savings	2,420	11.0	Commerce and housing
Deductibility of charitable contributions, other than education and health[c]	1,430	4.8	Education, training, employment, and social services
Energy production credit[d]	1,410	90.4	Energy
Special Employee Stock Ownership Plan rules	1,030	68.7	Income security
Excess of percentage over cost depletion, fuels	1,010	84.9	Energy
Expensing of research and experimentation expenditures	960	*	General science, space, and technology
Exclusion of interest on hospital construction bonds	900	29.0	Health

Tax expenditure	Estimated corporate revenue losses (dollars in millions)	Corporate share of total estimated revenue losses[a]	Budget function
Work opportunity tax credit	860	77.5	Education, training, employment, and social services
New markets tax credit	800	97.6	Community and regional development
Deductibility of charitable contributions (education)[c]	650	18.5	Education, training, employment, and social services
Exclusion of interest on bonds for private nonprofit educational facilities	610	29.0	Education, training, employment, and social services
Energy investment credit[d]	560	80.0	Energy
Excess of percentage over cost depletion, nonfuel minerals	550	94.8	Natural resources and environment
Alcohol fuel credits[e]	480	96.0	Energy
Tax incentives for preservation of historic structures	470	92.2	Natural resources and environment
Empowerment zones, the D.C. enterprise zone, and renewal communities	450	45.9	Community and regional development
Expensing of exploration and development costs, fuels	440	88.0	Energy
Advanced Energy Property Credit	390	90.7	Energy
Exclusion of interest on owner-occupied mortgage subsidy bonds	310	29.2	Commerce and housing
Credit for employee health insurance expenses of small business[f]	270	32.5	Health
Exclusion of interest on rental housing bonds	260	28.9	Commerce and housing
Exclusion of interest for airport, dock, and similar bonds	200	28.6	Community and regional development
Deductibility of charitable contributions (health)[c]	190	5.6	Health
Expensing of environmental remediation costs	170	85.0	Community and regional development
Expensing of multiperiod timber growing costs	160	64.0	Natural resources and environment
Exclusion of interest on student-loan bonds	140	29.2	Education, training, employment, and social services
Special rules for certain film and TV production	130	81.3	Commerce and housing
Tax credit for certain expenditures for maintaining railroad tracks	130	81.3	Transportation

(Continued)

Tax expenditure	Estimated corporate revenue losses (dollars in millions)	Corporate share of total estimated revenue losses[a]	Budget function
Exclusion of interest on bonds for water, sewage, and hazardous waste facilities	120	28.6	Natural resources and environment
Amortize all geological and geophysical expenditures over 2 years	100	83.3	Energy
Exclusion of interest on small issue bonds	70	29.2	Commerce and housing
Allowance of deduction for certain energy efficient commercial building property	60	75.0	Energy
Qualified school construction bonds[g]	60	28.6	Education, training, employment, and social services
Tribal Economic Development Bonds	60	35.3	Community and regional development
Exclusion of interest on bonds for Highway Projects and rail-truck transfer facilities	60	24.0	Transportation
Exclusion of gain or loss on sale or exchange of certain brownfield sites	40	66.7	Natural resources and environment
Tax credit and deduction for clean-fuel burning vehicles	40	44.4	Energy
Employee retention credit for employers in certain federal disaster areas	20	66.7	Education, training, employment, and social services
Credit to holders of Gulf Tax Credit Bonds.	20	25.0	Community and regional development
Credit for holding clean renewable energy bondsh	20	28.6	Energy
Credit for construction of new energy efficient homes	20	40.0	Energy
Exclusion of interest on energy facility bonds	10	50.0	Energy
Deduction for endangered species recovery expenditures	10	50.0	Natural resources and environment
Investment credit for rehabilitation of structures (other than historic)	10	50.0	Community and regional development
Credit for disabled access expenditures	10	50.0	Education, training, employment, and social services

Tax expenditure	Estimated corporate revenue losses (dollars in millions)	Corporate share of total estimated revenue losses[a]	Budget function
Exclusion of utility conservation subsidies	10	4.5	Energy
Expensing of certain multiperiod production costs	10	7.7	Agriculture
Expensing of reforestation expenditures	10	16.7	Agriculture
Accelerated depreciation on rental housing	(20)	14.3	Commerce and housing
Expensing of certain small investments	(40)	*	Commerce and housing
Accelerated depreciation of buildings other than rental housing	(3,300)	45.3%	Commerce and housing
Total	**$122,470**		

Source: GAO analysis of Office of Management and Budget budget data on tax expenditures, fiscal year 2013.

Note: Estimated revenue losses were negative for either corporations or individuals, meaning corporate revenue losses made up greater than 100 percent of the sum of both.

[a] The total includes estimated individual revenue losses.

[b] In addition, the credit for low-income housing investments has outlay effects of $3,480 million in 2011.

[c] Treasury estimates separate the deductibility of charitable contributions into three separate tax expenditures, deductibility for charitable contributions (health), deductibility for charitable contributions (education), deductibility for charitable contributions, other than health and education.

[d] Firms can request an energy grant in lieu of the energy production credit or the energy investment credit for facilities placed in service in 2009 and 2010 or whose construction commenced in 2009 and 2010. The effect of the grant on outlays was $3,510 million in 2011. See Office of Management and Budget, A*nalytical Perspectives, Budget of the United States Government, Fiscal Year 2013*, (Washington, D.C.: 2012).

[e] In addition, the alcohol fuel mixture credit results in a reduction in excise tax receipts of $6,520 million in 2011.

[f] In addition, the small business credit provision has outlay effects of $30 million in 2011.

[g] In addition, the provision for school construction bonds has outlay effects of $430 million in 2011.

[h] In addition, the provision has outlay effects of $20 million in 2011.

Appendix III. Twenty-Four Tax Expenditures with Only Estimated Corporate Revenue Losses Reported by Treasury, by Largest Estimated Corporate Revenue Losses, 2011

Tax expenditure	Estimated corporate revenue losses (dollars in millions)	Estimated revenue losses as a percentage of all corporate revenue losses	Budget function
Deferral of income from controlled foreign corporations	$41,410	22.82%	International affairs
Deferred taxes for financial firms on certain income earned overseas	6,180	3.41	International affairs
Graduated corporation income tax rate	3,280	1.81	Commerce and housing
Inventory property sales source rules exception	3,160	1.74	International affairs
Exemption of credit union income	1,110	0.61	Commerce and housing
Tax credit for orphan drug research	770	0.42	Health
Special Blue Cross/Blue Shield deduction	715	0.39	Health
Temporary 50 percent expensing for equipment used in the refining of liquid fuels	670	0.37	Energy
Credit for investment in clean coal facilities	370	0.20	Energy
Credit for energy efficient appliances	280	0.15	Energy
Tax exemption of certain insurance companies owned by tax-exempt organizations	200	0.11	Commerce and housing
Credit for holders of zone academy bonds[a]	200	0.11	Education, training, employment, and social services
Deferral of gain from dispositions of transmission property to implement Federal Energy Regulatory Commission restructuring policy	120	0.07	Energy

Tax expenditure	Estimated corporate revenue losses (dollars in millions)	Estimated revenue losses as a percentage of all corporate revenue losses	Budget function
Natural gas distribution pipelines treated as 15- year property	120	0.07	Energy
Exemption of certain mutuals' and cooperatives' income	110	0.06	Community and regional development
Expensing of exploration and development costs, nonfuel minerals	60	0.03	Natural resources and environment
Industrial carbon dioxide (CO_2) capture and sequestration tax credit	60	0.03	Natural resources and environment
Special alternative tax on small property and casualty insurance companies	40	0.02	Commerce and housing
Small life insurance company deduction	30	0.02	Commerce and housing
Bio-diesel and small agri-biodiesel producer tax credits[b]	20	0.01	Energy
Deferral of gain on sale of farm refiners	20	0.01	Agriculture
Deferral of tax on shipping companies[c]	20	0.01	Transportation
Alternative fuel production credit	10	0.01	Energy
Employer-provided child care credit	10	0.01	Education, training, employment, and social services
Total	**$58,965**	**32.50%**	

Source: GAO analysis of Office of Management and Budget budget data on tax expenditures, fiscal year 2013.

[a] In addition, the credit for holders of zone academy bonds had outlay effects totaling $10 million in 2011.

[b] In addition, the biodiesel producer tax credit results in a reduction in excise tax receipts of $760 million in 2011.

[c] These figures do not account for the tonnage tax which shipping companies may opt into in lieu of the corporate income tax. The tonnage tax reduces the cost of this tax expenditure by $20 per year in each year of the budget.

Appendix IV. Number of Corporate Taxpayer Recipients for Corporate-Only Tax Expenditures, 2010

Tax expenditure	Number of taxpayer recipients
Tax exemption of certain insurance companies owned by tax-exempt organizations	11,749[a]
Exemption of certain mutuals' and cooperatives' income[b]	6,996[a]
Exemption of credit union income[c]	3,570[a]
Special alternative tax on small property and casualty insurance companies[d]	1,812[a]
Bio-diesel and small agri-biodiesel producer tax credits	426
Small life insurance company deduction	325
Employer-provided child care credit	216
Tax credit for orphan drug research	99
Alternative fuel production credit	16[e]
Special Blue Cross/Blue Shield deduction	14
Credit for energy efficient appliances	5

Source: GAO analysis of Internal Revenue Service Statistics of Income Corporate Tax File Data estimates, 2010 and IRS Tax Exempt and Government Entities, Exempt Organizations, fiscal year 2011.

Note: Data on tax credits and deductions are from IRS SOI corporate file and includes active corporations that filed a return on forms 1120, 1120-F, 1120-L, and 1120-PC but not forms 1120S, 1120-REIT, and 1120-RIC. For two tax credits, IRS had data on the number of tax recipients but to avoid disclosure of specific taxpayers could not report this data because there were so few taxpayers claiming those tax credits. Based on the number of sampled returns and the coefficients of variation provided by Internal Revenue Service Statistics of Income, we estimate that the upper bound of a 95 percent confidence interval for the estimated total number is less than 830 corporations for the following tax expenditures: alternative fuel production credit, bio-diesel and small agri-biodiesel producer tax credits, credit for energy efficient appliances, employer-provided child care credit, tax credit for orphan drug research, small life insurance company deduction, and Special Blue Cross/Blue Shield deduction. Data on exemptions are from IRS Tax Exempt and Government Entities, Exempt Organizations division. Information from tax-exempt organization returns is available to the public and not subject to IRS disclosure regulations.

[a] Fiscal year 2010 data, Internal Revenue Service Tax Exempt and Government Entities, Exempt Organizations.

[b] Includes only benevolent life insurance associations.

[c] State chartered credit unions exempt from federal income tax under section 501(c) (14) (A) of the Internal Revenue Code are required to file an annual information returns while Federally chartered credits unions are tax exempt under section 501(c) (1) but are not required to file an annual information return and therefore Internal Revenue Service does not report the number of Federally chartered credit unions.

[d] Includes only mutual insurance companies.

[e] According to the Internal Revenue Service Statistics of Income division, estimate should be used with caution due to small number sampled returns claiming this credit.

APPENDIX V. REPORTED PURPOSE SUPPORTING A SPECIFIC ACTIVITY OR ENTITY FOR 24 CORPORATE-ONLY TAX EXPENDITURES

Number	Tax expenditure	Reported purpose
1	Inventory property sales source rules exception	Support for firms that produce goods domestically and export
2	Deferral of income from controlled foreign corporations	Support for firms that operate in foreign countries
3	Deferred taxes for financial firms on certain income earned overseas	Support for firms that operate in foreign countries
4	Alternative fuel production credit	Encourage production of nonconventional fuels
5	Bio-diesel and small agri-biodiesel producer tax credits	Encourage production of biodiesel fuels
6	Deferral of gain from dispositions of transmission property to implement Federal Energy Regulatory Commission restructuring policy	Support for independent transmission companies
7	Credit for investment in clean coal facilities	Encourage development of clean coal technologies
8	Temporary 50 percent expensing for equipment used in the refining of liquid fuels	Encourage development of fossil fuel refinery capacity
9	Natural gas distribution pipelines treated as 15-year property	Encourage development of natural gas pipeline infrastructure
10	Credit for energy efficient appliances	Encourage production of energy efficient appliances

(Continued)

Number	Tax expenditure	Reported purpose
11	Expensing of exploration and development costs, nonfuel minerals	Encourage nonfuel mineral exploration and development
12	Industrial carbon dioxide (CO^2) capture and sequestration tax credit	Encourage development of carbon capture and sequestration technologies
13	Deferral of gain on sale of farm refiners	Support to facilitate transfer of refiners and processors to farmers' cooperatives
14	Exemption of credit union income	Support for firms organized as credit unions
15	Special alternative tax on small property and casualty insurance companies	Support for small property and casualty insurance companies
16	Tax exemption of certain insurance companies owned by tax-exempt organizations	Support for insurance companies owned by tax-exempt organizations
17	Small life insurance company deduction	Support for small life insurance companies
18	Graduated corporation income tax rate	Support for small businesses and encourage corporate form of legal organization
19	Deferral of tax on shipping companies	Support for domestic shipbuilding and registry under U.S. flag
20	Exemption of certain mutuals' and cooperatives' income	Support for certain mutuals' and cooperatives' such as life insurance associations and telephone and electric companies
21	Credit for holders of zone academy bonds	Support for school renovation, equipment, teacher training, and course materials in economically distressed areas
22	Employer-provided child care credit	Encourage development of on-site employer child care facilities
23	Tax credit for orphan drug research	Encourage drug research and development for rare diseases
24	Special Blue Cross/Blue Shield deduction	Support for Blue Cross/Blue Shield organizations

Source: GAO analysis of Congressional Budget Office, Congressional Research Service, and GAO studies and legislative history.

Note: See appendix I for more detail on our methodology.

Appendix VI. Federal Activities That Appear to Share a Similar Purpose to 24 Corporate-Only Tax Expenditures

Number	Tax expenditure	Related federal activities	Administering agency	Type of assistance
1	Inventory property sales source rules exception	Export Guarantee Program	Department of Agriculture	Guaranteed/ insured loan
		Emerging Markets Program	Department of Agriculture	Direct payment
		Foreign Market Development Cooperator Program	Department of Agriculture	Direct payment
		Market Access Program	Department of Agriculture	Direct payment
		Technical Assistance for Specialty Crops Program	Department of Agriculture	Direct payment
		Quality Samples Program	Department of Agriculture	Direct payment
		CCC's Dairy Export Incentive Program	Department of Agriculture	Direct payment
2	Deferral of income from controlled foreign corporations	Deferred taxes for financial firms on certain income earned overseas	Internal Revenue Service	Deferral of tax
3	Deferred taxes for financial firms on certain income earned overseas	Deferral of income from controlled foreign corporations	Internal Revenue Service	Deferral of tax
4	Alternative fuel production credit	None identified	-	-
5	Bio-diesel and small agri-biodiesel producer tax credits	Bioenergy Program for Advanced Biofuels	Department of Agriculture	Direct payment
		Biorefinery Assistance	Department of Agriculture	Guaranteed/insured loan
		Integrated Biorefineries	Department of Energy	Grant

(Continued)

Number	Tax expenditure	Related federal activities	Administering agency	Type of assistance
6	Deferral of gain from dispositions of transmission property to implement Federal Energy Regulatory Commission restructuring policy	None identified	-	-
7	Credit for investment in clean coal facilities	Clean Coal Power Initiative	Department of Energy	Cooperative agreement
		Carbon Capture and Storage - FutureGen 2.0	Department of Energy	Cooperative agreement
		Industrial carbon dioxide (CO^2) capture and sequestration tax credit	Internal Revenue Service	Tax credit
		Qualified energy conservation bonds	Internal Revenue Service	Tax credit
		Advanced energy property credit	Internal Revenue Service	Tax credit
8	Temporary 50 percent expensing for equipment used in the refining of liquid fuels	None identified	-	-
9	Natural gas distribution pipelines treated as 15-year property	None identified	-	-
10	Credit for energy efficient appliances	Energy Efficient Appliance Rebate Program	Department of Energy	Grant

Number	Tax expenditure	Related federal activities	Administering agency	Type of assistance
		Building Technologies Program Appliance & Equipment Standards	Department of Energy	Regulation/standard
		Energy Star	Department of Energy/Environmental Protection Agency	Regulation/standard
11	Expensing of exploration and development costs, nonfuel minerals	Minerals Resources External Research Program	Department of the Interior	Cooperative agreement
		U.S. Geological Survey Research and Data Collection	Department of the Interior	Cooperative agreement
		Minerals and Mining on Indian Lands	Department of the Interior	Cooperative agreement and technical assistance
		Excess of percentage over cost depletion, nonfuel minerals	Internal Revenue Service	Tax exclusion, exemption, or deduction
12	Industrial carbon dioxide (CO2) capture and sequestration tax credit	Carbon Capture and Storage - FutureGen 2.0	Department of Energy	Cooperative agreement
		Industrial Carbon Capture and Storage (CCS) Application	Department of Energy	Cooperative agreement
		Credit for investment in clean coal facilities	Internal Revenue Service	Tax credit
		Qualified energy conservation bonds	Internal Revenue Service	Tax exclusion, exemption, or deduction
		Advanced energy property credit	Internal Revenue Service	Tax credit
		Geologic Sequestration of Carbon Dioxide	Environmental Protection Agency	Regulation/standard
13	Deferral of gain on sale of farm refiners	None identified	-	-

(Continued)

Number	Tax expenditure	Related federal activities	Administering agency	Type of assistance
14	Exemption of credit union income	None identified	-	-
15	Special alternative tax on small property and casualty insurance companies	None identified	-	-
16	Tax exemption of certain insurance companies owned by tax-exempt organizations	None identified	-	-
17	Small life insurance company deduction	None identified	-	-
18	Graduated corporation income tax rate	None identified	-	-
19	Deferral of tax on shipping companies	Federal Ship Financing Guarantees	Department of Transportation	Guaranteed/insured Loan
		Capital Construction Fund	Department of Transportation	Deferral of tax
		Construction Reserve Fund	Department of Transportation	Deferral of tax
		Assistance to Small Shipyards	Department of Transportation	Direct payment
		Fisheries Finance Program	Department of Commerce	Direct loan
20	Exemption of certain mutuals' and cooperatives' income	None identified	-	-
21	Credit for holders of zone academy bonds	Qualified school construction bonds	Internal Revenue Service	Tax credit

Number	Tax expenditure	Related federal activities	Administering agency	Type of assistance
22	Employer-provided child care credit	Employer provided child care exclusion	Internal Revenue Service	Tax exclusion, exemption, or deduction
23	Tax credit for orphan drug research	National Center for Advancing Translational Sciences	Department of Health and Human Services	Grant
		National Center for Research Resources	Department of Health and Human Services	Grant
24	Special Blue Cross/Blue Shield deduction	None identified	-	-

Source: GAO analysis of Catalog of Federal Domestic Assistance and agency documentation.

Note: The list of nontax programs we identified that appear to share a similar specific reported purpose has not been reviewed by the agencies responsible for them. See appendix I for more detail on our methodology.

End Notes

[1] GAO, *Tax Expenditures: Background and Evaluation Criteria and Questions*, GAO-13-167SP (Washington, D.C.: Nov. 29, 2012).

[2] The functional classification system is a way of grouping budgetary resources so that all budget authority and outlays of on-budget and off-budget federal entities and tax expenditures can be presented according to the national needs being addressed. National needs are grouped in 18 broad areas to provide a coherent and comprehensive basis for analyzing and understanding the budget. See GAO, *A Glossary of Terms Used in the Federal Budget Process*, GAO-05-734SP (Washington, D.C.: Sept. 1, 2005).

[3] While sufficiently reliable as a gauge of general magnitude, summing revenue loss estimates does not take into account any interactions between tax expenditures. In addition, revenue loss estimates do not incorporate any behavioral responses and, thus, do not represent the revenue amount that would be gained if a specific tax expenditure was repealed. For further discussion on summing of tax expenditure estimates and examples, see GAO, *Government Performance and Accountability: Tax Expenditures Represent a Substantial Federal Commitment and Need to Be Reexamined*, GAO-05-690 (Washington, D.C.: Sept. 23, 2005).

[4] Tax expenditures may be available to corporate and individual taxpayers, including other types of business entities other than corporations. Treasury estimates the portion of revenue losses associated with corporate or individual taxpayers for each tax expenditure in its list. According to Treasury's estimates, some tax expenditures may be used by only corporate taxpayers and some by only individual taxpayers while other tax expenditures may be used by both corporate and individual taxpayers.

[5] When the number of taxpayers claiming a tax expenditure is small, even with a large sample such as the IRS SOI corporate sample, estimates for small subpopulations like these often have large confidence intervals. For three of the corporate-only tax expenditures, the estimated number of corporations claiming the expenditure was less than 17. See appendix I for additional detail on the IRS SOI corporate sample.

[6] Office of Management and Budget, *Analytical Perspectives, Budget of the United States Government, Fiscal Year 2013*, (Washington, D.C.: 2012) and U.S. Congress, Senate Committee on the Budget, *Tax Expenditures: Compendium of Background Material on Individual Provisions*, S. Prt. 111-58. Prepared by CRS (Washington, D.C.: December 2010).

[7] The concept of tax expenditures extends beyond the income tax. Tax expenditures also exist for other types of taxes, such as excise and payroll taxes. For more detail on the normal structure of tax expenditures, see pg. 92 of GAO, *Government Performance and Accountability: Tax Expenditures Represent a Substantial Federal Commitment and Need to Be Reexamined*, GAO-05-690 (Washington, D.C.: Sept. 23, 2005).

[8] Pub. L. No. 93-344, §3, 88 Stat. 297, 299 (July 12, 1974) (*codified at* 2 U.S.C. § 622(3)). Provisions must be compared to a "normal structure," or baseline, and the Congressional Budget and Impoundment Control Act did not define a specific baseline structure.

[9] Office of Management and Budget, *Analytical Perspectives, Budget of the United States Government, Fiscal Year 2013*, (Washington, D.C.: 2012); and Joint Committee on Taxation, *Estimates of Federal Tax Expenditures for Fiscal Years 2011-2015*, JCS-1-12, (Washington, D.C.: Jan. 17, 2012).

[10] While, in general, the tax expenditure lists Treasury and the Joint Committee on Taxation publish annually are similar, they differ somewhat in the number of tax expenditures reported and the estimated revenue losses for particular expenditures because the organizations use different (1) income tax baselines; (2) de minimis amounts, which is the minimum revenue loss threshold for Treasury and the Joint Committee on Taxation to report a tax expenditure; and (3) economic and technical assumptions. For more information

on how Treasury and the Joint Committee on Taxation estimate revenue loss, see appendix III of GAO-05-690.

[11] S corporations are limited to no more than 100 shareholders and can only issue one class of stock. See CRS, *Business Organizational Choices: Taxation and Response to Legislative Changes*, (Washington, D.C.: Apr. 26, 2012).

[12] Limited liability companies, business entities organized under state law, are treated under IRS default rules as partnerships or disregarded entities, depending on the number of members. If a limited liability company chooses not to be classified under the default classification, it can elect to be taxed as a C corporation or S corporation. Under the last option the company's income and expenses are simply attributed to its parent corporation. See GAO, *Business Tax Reform: Simplification and Increased Uniformity of Taxation Would Yield Benefits*, GAO-06-1113T (Washington, D.C.: Sept. 20, 2006).

[13] See Tax Policy Center, *How Big Are Total Individual Income Tax Expenditures, and Who Benefits from Them*? Discussion Paper No. 31 (December 2008) and GAO, *Understanding the Tax Reform Debate: Background, Criteria, & Questions*, GAO-05-1009SP (Washington, D.C.: Sept. 1, 2005).

[14] See IRS SOI, *Corporation Complete Report*. This data includes active corporations that filed a return on forms 1120, 1120-A (until 2006), 1120-F, 1120-L, and 1120-PC but not forms 1120S, 1120-REIT, and 1120- RIC.

[15] Trends in the number of and estimated revenue losses for corporate tax expenditures are discussed later in this report.

[16] GAO, *Tax Expenditures: Background and Evaluation Criteria and Questions*, GAO-13-167SP (Washington, D.C.: Nov. 29, 2012).

[17] GAO, *Government Performance and Accountability: Tax Expenditures Represent a Substantial Federal Commitment and Need to Be Reexamined*, GAO-05-690 (Washington, D.C.: Sept. 23, 2005), and *Tax Policy: Tax Expenditures Deserve More Scrutiny*, GAO/GGD/AIMD-94-122 (Washington, D.C.: June 3, 1994).

[18] Pub. L. No. 111-352, 124 Stat. 3866 (Jan. 4, 2011).

[19] GAO, *Managing for Results: Opportunities for Congress to Address Government Performance Issues*, GAO-12-215R (Washington, D.C.: Dec. 9, 2011) and *Managing for Results: GPRA Modernization Act Implementation Provides Important Opportunities to Address Government Challenges*, GAO-11-617T (Washington, D.C.: May 10, 2011).

[20] The number of tax expenditures reflects all provisions reported by Treasury, including those enacted but effective for future fiscal years. Some provisions listed by Treasury as one tax expenditure may actually include multiple tax provisions aggregated together. In addition, fluctuations in the trend lines from year-to-year may reflect changes in Treasury's methodology rather than changes in tax law enacted.

[21] In addition, the alcohol fuel mixture credit also results in a reduction in excise tax receipts of $6.52 billion in 2011 according to Treasury's estimates.

[22] According to Treasury officials, two of the corporate-only tax expenditures are limited to C corporations or those treated as C corporations by the Internal Revenue Code. These tax expenditures include the graduated corporation income tax rate, which applies only to corporations, and the credit for holders of zone academy bonds, which is available only to certain types of corporations investing in school construction. See 26 U.S.C. §§ 11, 54E, 1397E. Four additional tax expenditures are restricted to corporations even though the recipients may not be organized as corporations. The Internal Revenue Code requires insurance companies to file as C corporations for federal corporate income tax purposes irrespective of their legal form of organization (sec. 7701(a)(3)). Treasury also assumes for two tax expenditures that all organizations claiming the tax expenditure would file their tax returns under the federal corporate income tax system if the tax expenditure was removed. The remaining 16 tax expenditures could be used by individuals and "pass- through" entities. Treasury estimated that these tax expenditures had 2011 revenue losses only for

corporations or that the estimated individual revenue losses were less than Treasury's de minimus reporting threshold of $5 million.

[23] For the number of recipients claiming tax expenditures, tax exemption data are fiscal year 2010 data while tax credit and deduction data is 2010 corporate tax year data. For corporate tax expenditures, the corporations may not be the sole or ultimate beneficiaries intended to benefit from the special tax treatment. For example, in addition to the manufacturers directly claiming the credit for energy efficient appliances, consumers would benefit from any increased supply and lower prices for energy efficient appliances.

[24] GAO, *Renewable Energy: Federal Agencies Implement Hundreds of Initiatives*, GAO-12-260 (Washington, D.C.: Feb. 27, 2012).

[25] Although the tax expenditure concept can also be applied to other kinds of taxes, such as excise taxes, this report only covers tax expenditures for the federal income tax system. Tax expenditures may be available to corporate and individual taxpayers, including other types of business entities other than corporations. Treasury estimates the portion of revenue losses associated with corporate or individual taxpayers for each tax expenditure in its list. According to Treasury's estimates, some tax expenditures may be used by only corporate taxpayers and some by only individual taxpayers while other tax expenditures may be used by both corporate and individual taxpayers.

[26] The number of tax expenditures reflects all provisions reported by Treasury, including those enacted but effective for future fiscal years. Some provisions listed by Treasury as one tax expenditure may actually include multiple tax provisions aggregated together. In addition, fluctuations in the trend lines from year-to-year may reflect changes in Treasury's methodology rather than changes in tax law enacted. See GAO-05-690.

[27] For further discussion on summing of tax expenditure estimates and examples, see GAO, *Government Performance and Accountability: Tax Expenditures Represent a Substantial Federal Commitment and Need to Be Reexamined*, GAO-05-690 (Washington, D.C.: Sept. 23, 2005).

[28] In the fiscal year 2013 *Analytical Perspectives*, Treasury listed 173 tax expenditures. Three tax expenditures listed by Treasury did not have estimates for corporations or individuals in 2011 but did have estimates in future fiscal years and three tax expenditures had no estimates for corporations or individuals in any of the estimated fiscal years. Some of the tax expenditures identified as having corporate revenue losses in 2011 may have expired at the end of calendar year 2011 or 2012.

[29] Federal tax information—tax returns and return information—are kept confidential under section 6103 of the Internal Revenue Code except as specifically authorized by Congress. Section 6103 specifies what federal tax information can be disclosed, to whom, and for what purposes.

[30] When the number of taxpayers claiming a tax expenditure is small, even with a large sample such as the IRS SOI corporate sample, estimates for small subpopulations like these often have large confidence intervals. For three of the corporate-only tax expenditures, the estimated number of corporations claiming the expenditure was less than 17.

[31] U.S. Congress, Senate Committee on the Budget, *Tax Expenditures: Compendium of Background Material on Individual Provisions*, S. Prt. 111-58. Prepared by CRS (Washington, D.C.: December 2010).

[32] We used one prior GAO report as an example of the historical rationale of one corporate tax expenditure. See GAO, *Financial Institutions: Issues Regarding the Tax-Exempt Status of Credit Unions*, GAO-06-220T (Washington, D.C: Nov. 3. 2005).

[33] Office of Management and Budget, *Analytical Perspectives, Budget of the United States Government, Fiscal Year 2013*, (Washington, D.C.: 2012) and U.S. Congress, Senate Committee on the Budget, *Tax Expenditures: Compendium of Background Material on Individual Provisions*, S. Prt. 111-58. Prepared by CRS (Washington, D.C.: December 2010). Treasury's and CRS's tax expenditure lists were generally similar as CRS's relies on upon the Joint Committee on Taxation's tax expenditure list.

[34] We obtained data from IRS for the tax expenditures identified as related, from the Department of Energy for the Integrated Biorefineries Program, and for the standards and regulations identified as related from the Department of Energy and the Environmental Protection Agency.

In: Corporate Taxes
Editor: Brianne Nathanson

ISBN: 978-1-63321-922-9

Chapter 2

CORPORATE TAX EXPENDITURES: EVALUATIONS OF TAX DEFERRALS AND GRADUATED TAX RATES*

United States Government Accountability Office

WHY GAO DID THIS STUDY

Congress and the administration are reexamining tax expenditures used by corporations as part of corporate tax reform. These tax expenditures— special exemptions and exclusions, credits, deductions, deferrals, and preferential tax rates—support federal policy goals, but result in revenue forgone by the federal government.

GAO was asked to examine issues related to certain tax expenditures. This report uses GAO's tax expenditures evaluation guide to determine what is known about: (1) the deferral of income for controlled foreign corporations; (2) deferred taxes for certain financial firms on income earned overseas; and (3) the graduated corporate income tax rate. GAO combined the two deferral provisions for evaluation purposes.

GAO's guide suggests using five questions to evaluate a tax expenditure: (1) what is its purpose and is the purpose being achieved; (2) does it meet the criteria for good tax policy; (3) how is it related to other federal programs; (4)

* This is an edited, reformatted and augmented version of a United States Government Accountability Office publication, No. GAO-13-789, dated September 2013.

what are its consequences for the federal budget; and (5) how is its evaluation being managed? To address these questions, GAO reviewed the legislative history and relevant academic and government studies, analyzed 2010 Internal Revenue Service (IRS) data, and interviewed agency officials and tax experts.

What GAO Recommends

GAO made no recommendations. Treasury, IRS, the Joint Committee on Taxation, and external experts provided technical comments that were incorporated, as appropriate.

What GAO Found

Deferral: Both deferral tax expenditures confer the benefit of effectively reducing taxes by delaying the taxation of certain income of foreign subsidiaries of U.S. corporations until it is repatriated to the U.S. parent as dividends.

1) While views on the purpose of deferral have changed over time, currently, it is often viewed by experts as promoting the competitiveness of U.S. multinational corporations. Some experts argue that this view is too narrow. For example, this definition of competitiveness ignores the effect on other corporations that cannot use deferral, such as those that are purely domestic or export without foreign subsidiaries. Further, it ignores impacts on the wider economy.
2) Good tax policy has several dimensions. By delaying the tax on foreign source income, deferral could distort corporate investment and location decisions in a way that lower taxes, but favor less productive activities over more productive ones. Informed judgments about deferral's effect on the fairness of the tax system cannot be made because who benefits from deferral, after accounting for such factors as changes in prices and wages, has not been determined. However, there is widespread agreement among experts and the Internal Revenue Service (IRS) that deferral adds complexity to the tax code.

3) GAO did not identify other federal spending programs that provide similar support to U.S. multinational corporations.
4) Joint Committee on Taxation (JCT) 2011 estimates show relatively modest consequences for the federal budget.
5) No federal agency has been tasked with evaluating deferral.

Graduated corporate income tax rate schedule: The graduated tax rates lower tax rates for corporations with less than $10 million in taxable income.

1) The purpose of the graduated corporate income tax rate schedule is viewed by the sources GAO reviewed as supporting small businesses. However, evidence is mixed on whether it achieves this purpose. The tax rates may not be well targeted toward supporting small businesses because corporations that are large in terms of assets and gross receipts may have taxable income that is small enough to qualify for the rates.
2) The economic efficiency of the graduated rates depends on whether they correct for a market failure. This includes too few small businesses forming, given their potential for profit and innovation, which offsets the possible distortions from its advantaging one type of business organization over others. GAO did not identify any studies of the efficiency effects or those that specifically estimate the distribution of the benefits from the graduated rates. According to IRS staff, while the graduated rates present little complexity, some evidence of tax planning to avoid higher rates has been found.
3) The graduated rates may be related to a number of federal spending programs also targeted to small businesses.
4) JCT 2011 estimates also show modest consequences for the federal budget.
5) No federal agency has been tasked with evaluating the graduated rates.

ABBREVIATIONS

BEA	Bureau of Economic Analysis
CBO	Congressional Budget Office
CRS	Congressional Research Service
FTC	Foreign Tax Credit

IRC	Internal Revenue Code
IRS	Internal Revenue Service
JCT	Joint Committee on Taxation
OMB	Office of Management and Budget
SOI	Statistics of Income
Treasury	Department of the Treasury

* * *

September 16, 2013

The Honorable John Lewis
Ranking Member
Committee on Ways and Means
Subcommittee on Oversight
United States House of Representatives

The Honorable Lloyd Doggett
United States House of Representatives

In the past few years, both Congress and the administration have proposed reforming the corporate income tax system. A key component of discussions about reform is determining how the income of U.S. multinational corporations should be taxed—in particular, whether the federal government should continue or modify the current deferral of taxes on certain income until it is repatriated back to the United States. Currently, there are two provisions that relate to the deferral of U.S. taxation of foreign-source income: a general provision that applies to all controlled foreign corporations and a special provision applicable to active financial-services income. Another key component of reform discussions is the appropriate corporate income tax rate and structure. The current structure includes a set of graduated tax rates. The Department of the Treasury (Treasury) identifies both deferral provisions and the graduated rates as corporate tax expenditures because they are reductions in the federal corporate income tax liability that result from special provisions of the tax code. As our prior work pointed out, these tax expenditures are among the largest utilized only by corporate taxpayers.[1] According to Treasury's estimates, the amount of corporate tax revenue forgone from these three tax expenditures totaled almost $49 billion in fiscal year 2012.[2] Modifying or eliminating these tax expenditures as part of corporate tax reform will likely involve tradeoffs between various objectives pursued by the federal government, such as tax revenue and corporate investment.

Because of your ongoing interest in whether and how well these tax expenditures are achieving their purposes, you requested that we apply the guide that we recently developed for evaluating the performance of tax expenditures to certain corporate ones. 3 This report uses our guide to determine what is known about the following three tax expenditures: (1) the deferral of income for controlled foreign corporations; (2) deferred taxes for certain financial firms on income earned overseas; and (3) the graduated corporate income tax rate.

Because the two deferral provisions are so similar, we combine them for evaluation purposes, and then evaluate the graduated rates separately.

Our tax expenditure evaluation guide outlines a series of questions and criteria that can be used to evaluate tax expenditures. The five primary questions outlined in the guide are:

1) What is the tax expenditure's purpose and is it being achieved?
2) Even if its purpose is achieved, is the tax expenditure good policy?
    a) Does it generate net economic benefits for society?
    b) Is it fair?
    c) Is it simple, transparent, and administrable?
3) How does the tax expenditure relate to other federal programs?
4) What are the consequences for the federal budget of the tax expenditure?
5) How should evaluation of the tax expenditure be managed?

The guide's questions cover a number of different policy objectives, which sometimes compete with one another. This report provides information in response to the questions, but does not attempt to balance the different objectives or make recommendations. Rather, policymakers are in the best position to judge how competing policy objectives should be weighed.

As we note in our tax expenditure evaluation guide, the guide is not a "one size fits all" framework for evaluating tax expenditures. We used reasonable judgment in applying the guide's questions and concepts to evaluate the three tax expenditures. In some instances, we focused our discussion on certain questions in the guide because they were more relevant to the tax expenditures we were evaluating. At the same time, we devoted less discussion to other questions that were more technical in nature. See appendix I for the guide's full list of questions.

To determine what is known with respect to the deferral tax expenditures and the graduated corporate income tax rate schedule, we reviewed a variety of sources. These sources included studies by GAO, the Congressional Research Service (CRS), the Congressional Budget Office (CBO), the Joint Committee on Taxation (JCT), and other federal agencies; legislation, statutes, and regulations related to each of the tax expenditures; and academic research. We also interviewed officials at Treasury, the Internal Revenue Service (IRS), and three external experts, one from CRS and two from universities, who have researched and written extensively on the U.S. corporate income tax system. The results from these interviews are not generalizable. When no consensus existed among our sources for the answer to a question, we summarized the debate and provided citations for the various views. We analyzed Treasury's tax expenditure estimates from 1998 to 2012, and 2011 estimates by JCT on the revenue effects of changing tax expenditures. We also analyzed 2010 data from the IRS Statistics of Income (SOI), the most recent year available at the time of our work, and data from the Bureau of Economic Analysis (BEA) that covered 1987 to 2012. To assess the reliability of the data and estimates, we reviewed agency documentation, interviewed agency officials, and reviewed our prior reports that have used them. We determined that the Treasury, BEA, JCT, and IRS data and estimates were sufficiently reliable for our purposes.[4]

We conducted our work from April to September 2013 in accordance with all sections of GAO's Quality Assurance Framework that are relevant to our objectives. The framework requires that we plan and perform the engagement to obtain sufficient and appropriate evidence to meet our stated objectives, and to discuss any limitations in our work. We believe that the information and data obtained, and the analysis conducted, provide a reasonable basis for any findings and conclusions in this product.

BACKGROUND

The United States taxes domestic corporations on their worldwide income, regardless of where it is earned, and provides credits for foreign income taxes paid. A U.S. parent corporation may directly or indirectly own multiple corporations, including both domestic and foreign subsidiaries. The U.S. taxes the worldwide income of U.S. corporations, whether earned domestically or abroad. However, the active business income earned by foreign subsidiaries is generally eligible for deferral from U.S. tax until it is distributed, usually in the form of dividends, to the U.S. parent corporation or other U.S. shareholders.[5]

When income is repatriated in this way, it may have already been taxed in the foreign country where it was earned. To avoid taxing foreign source income twice, the federal tax code allows U.S. parent corporations a foreign tax credit (FTC) for taxes paid to other countries. A U.S. corporation would pay U.S. tax on foreign-source income only to the extent that the U.S. tax on that income exceeds the FTC. Figure 1 shows how deferral affects how a dividend payment from a foreign subsidiary to its U.S. parent corporation is generally taxed under the U.S. worldwide tax approach.

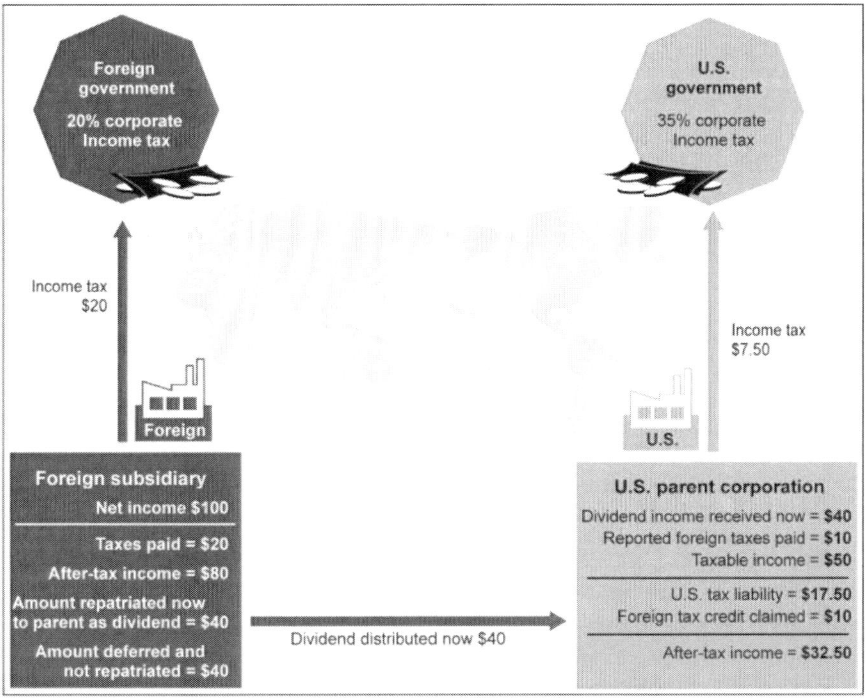

Source: GAO analysis.

Figure 1. Example of Deferral under the U.S. Worldwide Corporate Income Tax System.

Passive income, such as dividends, interest, rental income, and royalties received by controlled foreign corporations, and certain types of easily manipulated active income, is not subject to deferral.[6] Income ineligible for deferral is defined under Subpart F of the Internal Revenue Code (IRC).

Unlike the United States, most developed countries do not tax corporations on their worldwide income. Instead, these countries use a territorial tax system that taxes only the income earned within a country's physical borders, and exempts from tax dividends received from foreign subsidiaries on their foreign earnings as well as gains realized on the sale of foreign subsidiaries. There has been a trend of developed countries moving towards territorial tax systems. As of 2012, 28 of the 34 current member countries of the Organisation for Economic Co-operation and Development have adopted some form of a territorial tax system.[7] However, most countries generally do not use a pure form of either the worldwide (also known as a full-inclusion system) or territorial tax system. Rather, countries tend to use a hybrid system that contains some features of both systems. For example, the deferral provisions in the U.S. worldwide system delay the taxation of foreign source income, whereas a purer form of the worldwide system would tax this income as it is earned. As we have previously found, countries using the territorial approach do not exempt all foreign source income from taxation, but have exceptions for certain types of passive income.[8]

The income of controlled foreign corporations that is generated through the primary business activities related to financial-services is excepted from Subpart F's anti-deferral regime. Interest income, for example, which would typically fall under the Subpart F definition, and thus would be taxed currently whether or not it is repatriated to a U.S. parent corporation, is permitted to be deferred under this active financial-services income provision. This tax expenditure is an exception to Subpart F because it treats what would otherwise be considered passive income as active business income that can be deferred since it was earned through the primary business activities of financial-services companies. The effect of the exception is to include financial-services companies among the U.S. corporations that can defer taxation on their business income earned abroad.

The United States taxes all foreign and domestic corporate income using a graduated corporate income tax rate structure. Corporations with less than $10 million in net taxable corporate income are subject to different tax rates, depending on the amount of income earned. As seen in table 1, income is taxed at graduated rates of 15, 25, 39, and 34 percent for various income levels up to $10 million, and 35 and 38 percent for income up to $18,333,333. The 38- and 39-percent rates reduce the benefits provided by the lower graduated rates.[9] Finally, for corporations with taxable income higher than $18,333,333, a flat rate of 35 percent applies to all taxable income.

Table 1. Corporate Income Tax Rate Schedule

Taxable Income over	But not over...	Tax rate	Of the amount over...
$0	$50,000	15%	$0
$50,000	$75,000	$7,500 + 25%	$50,000
$75,000	$100,000	13,750 + 34%	$75,000
$100,000	$355,000	22,250 + 39%	$100,000
$335,000	$10,000,000	113,900 + 34%	$335,000
$10,000,000	$15,000,000	3,400,000 + 35%	$10,000,000
$15,000,000	$18,333,333	5,150,000 + 38%	$15,000,000
$18,333,333	-	35%	0

Source: Internal Revenue Service.

Treasury and JCT designate the two deferral provisions and the graduated corporate income tax rate schedule as tax expenditures because they are special tax provisions that are exceptions to the normal structure of the corporate income tax system.[10] The deferral provisions are designated as tax expenditures because they deviate from the baseline case of a pure worldwide tax system in which U.S. corporations would be taxed on their worldwide income whether or not the income is repatriated to the United States. The graduated rate provision is designated a tax expenditure because it is an exception to the normal structure of a flat corporate income tax rate. All three tax expenditures reduce revenue received by the federal government below what it would be under the normal structure established by Treasury and JCT.[11]

Treasury and JCT each compile an annual list of tax expenditures by budget function with estimates of the corporate and individual income tax revenue losses, also known as tax expenditure estimates.[12] They separately calculate the estimated revenue losses for each tax expenditure under the assumptions that all other tax expenditures remain in the tax code, and taxpayer behavior remains constant.[13] Thus, the tax expenditure estimates do not represent the amount of revenue that would be gained if a particular tax expenditure was repealed, since repeal would probably change taxpayer behavior in some way that would affect revenue.

EVALUATION OF TAX DEFERRALS

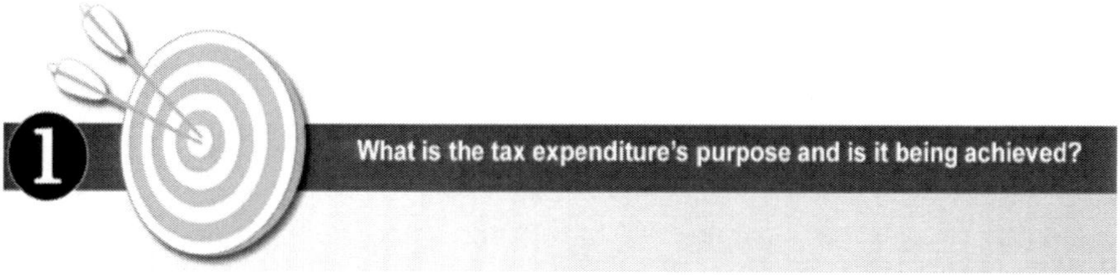

Deferral Is Viewed by Many as Promoting Competitiveness

Deferral has long been a part of the tax code, and views of its purpose have changed over time. Currently, it is often viewed by tax experts and in the research that we reviewed as promoting competitiveness.[14] However, deferral's effect on competitiveness depends on how competitiveness is defined. If competitiveness refers to the ability of U.S. multinational corporations to operate successfully in foreign markets through their subsidiaries, then deferral, which increases after tax returns by delaying tax payments, provides a benefit that may enhance competitiveness.[15] In foreign markets, U.S. corporations face competitors that, operating under a territorial tax system in their own countries, pay tax only in the foreign country. U.S. corporations under the worldwide system must pay the foreign tax plus any U.S. tax on the same income. By delaying this U.S. tax, deferral is said to move U.S. corporations closer to having a "level playing field" with their foreign competitors.

Whether the tax benefit provided by deferral results in net positive economic effects for the United States is the subject of debate. Some research has found that investments U.S. multinationals make abroad, due in part to the incentives provided by deferral, lead to positive economic effects for employment and wages in the United States, while others have questioned the magnitude of these effects.[16] Treasury officials noted that in some instances U.S. foreign direct investment may be associated with increased investment in the United States. In other instances, it may be associated with decreased U.S. investment, meaning that the effect on employment and wages in the United States would be uncertain.

However, whether this definition of competitiveness that focuses on multinationals is appropriate has been a subject of debate among experts.[17] Competitiveness has also been defined as the ability of U.S. corporations to operate successfully in domestic markets, and to export products into foreign markets. Deferral provides no benefit to these purely domestic or exporting U.S corporations. Rather than leveling the playing field, deferral benefits U.S. multinationals over other types of U.S. corporations.[18] Our prior work has shown that deferral and other aspects of U.S. international corporate taxation allow U.S. multinational corporations to pay a much smaller U.S. effective tax rate on foreign source income than domestic income.[19] If these multinationals earn income in countries that, on average, have lower corporate tax rates than the United States, they have an advantage over purely domestic U.S. corporations because the average effective tax rate on the multinationals' worldwide income may be lower than the rate paid by the purely domestic corporations on their U.S. income. However, there is some research that has found that multinationals and domestic-only firms face similar effective tax rates.[20]

Other tax experts argue that the appropriate definition of competitiveness should focus on broader industry or national purposes rather than corporations.[21] For example, a U.S. industry is said to be more competitive by attracting more investment and resources than foreign industries.[22] For others, competitiveness is a more general concept, referring to the set of institutions, policies, and human and natural endowments that make a country productive. A tax policy that promotes competitiveness under this definition would try to assure that the tax system does not prevent a country's resources from being put to their most productive uses.[23] Countries that meet this standard can engage most effectively in international trade that can be mutually beneficial. Tax benefits for only certain corporations or industries may not meet this criterion. Finally, some experts note that the concept of competitiveness is the wrong concept to focus on when formulating tax policy and that efficiency, which we discuss in the following section, is the appropriate concept. They argue that simply using the wrong concept in this way leads to bad policy outcomes.[24]

Even if its purpose is achieved, is the tax expenditure good policy?

- **Does the tax expenditure generate net economic benefits for society?**
- Is the tax expenditure fair?
- Is the tax expenditure simple, transparent, and administrable?

Tax differences between countries can affect decisions made by multinational corporations, including where to invest in operations, where to locate their corporate residences, when to repatriate income from foreign subsidiaries, and whether to acquire foreign or domestic corporations. Their decisions are said to be distorted when the corporations respond to tax differences by putting resources into less productive activities because these activities are taxed less heavily than more productive uses. As we stated in our guide, when this happens, the economy is not as productive as it could be, and society does not achieve as high a standard of living as it would if the distortion did not exist.[25]

Numerous Business Decisions Are Affected by Deferral and Each Has Consequences for Efficiency

As mentioned above, the United States uses a hybrid form of the worldwide tax system where deferral delays but does not eliminate the U.S. tax on foreign source income. In this way, the U.S. worldwide system has some features less like a pure worldwide system and more like a territorial system. Moving in either direction would affect deferral. On one hand, the United States could eliminate deferral if it moved towards a more pure worldwide system by adopting a full inclusion system where foreign source income is taxed by the United States as it is earned rather than when it is repatriated. On the other hand, the United States could move towards a more territorial system by exempting foreign source income from U.S. taxation, or, in effect, making deferral permanent.[26] The effect on corporations' decision making and ultimately on efficiency will depend on which way of ending deferral is adopted. The following discusses some of the decisions that have been identified in the literature where deferral could increase or decrease distortions.

Some tax experts argue that deferral may distort decisions about where U.S. corporations invest, compared to a full-inclusion system, if the U.S. tax rate is higher than foreign tax rates, as is often the case. This difference in tax rates, combined with the ability to defer paying the higher U.S. tax until income is repatriated, could mean that a U.S. corporation earns more after taxes from a less productive investment abroad than from a more productive investment at home. The efficiency loss is the loss of income (or product) that results when the corporation chooses the less productive foreign investment because it produces a higher after-tax return. Some research has shown that differences in tax burden do affect corporations' real investment decisions, which could lead to these efficiency losses. [27] If the United States adopted a full inclusion system, this distortion affecting the allocation of investment domestically or abroad could potentially be reduced because the tax incentive to invest abroad would be eliminated, since corporations would pay the same U.S. tax on their worldwide income, whether it comes from foreign or domestic investments. Under a territorial system, these investment location distortions may increase relative to the current system because the tax incentive to invest in low-tax countries may be enhanced when the differences in tax rates are made permanent. However, the responsiveness of investment decisions to tax rate differences indicates that U.S. corporations could be at a disadvantage under a full inclusion system as they could be competing against foreign companies which would likely be taxed under a territorial tax system and at a lower tax rate. This disadvantage would be removed under a territorial system where U.S. corporations would face the same tax rate as foreign competitors also operating in those countries.

Some experts and research that we reviewed argue that deferral may reduce distortions, compared to a full inclusion system, about where businesses decide to incorporate, and whether U.S. corporations choose to change their country of incorporation to a foreign country (so-called corporate inversions). By choosing not to have its corporate residence in the U.S., a corporation could permanently avoid U.S. tax on income earned abroad, and whatever income it is able to shift out of the U.S. Deferral may somewhat reduce this distortion by allowing corporations to defer from tax income earned abroad. Some research has indicated that taxing income, once it is repatriated, affects decisions of where to incorporate, or to change incorporation from one country to another.[28] Some research has also shown that most inversions that occur for tax reasons are to avoid U.S. tax on income earned in the U.S. by increasing the scope for income shifting rather than to avoid U.S. tax on foreign-source income.[29] However, recent research has found mixed results on trends in the number of inversions. Some have found that only a small number of U.S. corporations that conduct initial public offerings have reincorporated in low-tax countries, while others have recently highlighted an increase in inversions.[30] In 2004, legislation was passed to limit the ability of U.S. corporations to change their country of incorporation to a foreign country.[31] This corporate residence distortion could be increased by full inclusion, which would raise the effective U.S. tax on income earned abroad, and encourage companies to avoid this tax by moving their residence abroad. A territorial system would eliminate this incentive by removing the U.S. tax on foreign source income.

It is also argued that deferral, compared to a full inclusion system, improves economic efficiency by removing distortions that affect decisions about which subsidiaries and other assets corporations own.[32] Some corporate groups may be able to use foreign subsidiaries and assets more productively because of synergies that result from ownership within the corporate group, while another corporate group that acquired these subsidiaries and assets would not have these synergies and therefore would not be able to use them as productively. For this reason, tax differences could lead to productivity loss when a corporation without those synergies, but with more favorable tax treatment is able to outbid for ownership of those assets a corporation with those synergies. In this case, the use of deferral or a territorial system makes inefficiency less likely and the move to full inclusion makes it more likely. However, others argue that ownership synergies do not have significant effects on productivity because there are numerous ways for corporations to use assets as productively without owning them, such as leasing, contract manufacturing, or licensing of trademarks or technology.[33] In this case, deferral or a move to a territorial system would not produce significant efficiency gains.

Some research has also shown that deferral can distort decision making by affecting the timing of repatriations, referred to as the "lockout" effect. The distortion would happen if deferral incentivizes corporations to keep income abroad rather than repatriating it to the higher tax country. This income may be more productive if repatriated and reinvested at home rather than retained (or "locked out") abroad for tax reasons. Although estimates have varied over time, they consistently show that the lockout effect does have efficiency costs. Estimates from 2001 of the efficiency cost of U.S. multinational corporations from the lockout effect put the size of the loss at about 1 percent of foreign pretax income. 34 However, the large repatriations under the 2004 tax holiday have suggested to some researchers that these earlier estimates may be too small.[35] More recent estimates have shown that the efficiency loss increases with the amount of earnings accumulated abroad, and could be as high as 7 percent of foreign pretax income by 2015.[36] Both the territorial and full inclusion systems eliminate the lockout effect. The territorial system makes foreign earnings tax free whether or not they are repatriated, and the full inclusion system makes foreign earnings taxable without repatriation.

The extensive literature on deferral disagrees on its overall impact on efficiency, or whether a movement toward a full inclusion or territorial system would improve efficiency. Deferral's effect on the decisions just discussed, where to invest, where to locate headquarters, whether to make an acquisition, and when to repatriate income can depend on factors such as the location of the market (domestic or foreign) and the source of investment capital (again, domestic or foreign). In addition, there may be empirical disagreement about the size of an effect. Without agreement on the separate effects on efficiency, there is no agreement about how to add them up to get an overall effect.

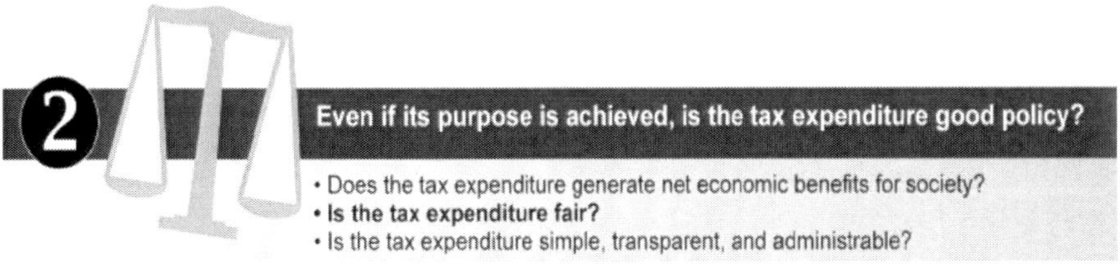

Informed Judgments about Deferral's Equity Require Information about Ultimate Beneficiaries

We were unable to find any studies that specifically estimate the distribution of the benefits from the two deferral tax expenditures. Treasury, CBO, and the Tax Policy Center have developed estimates of the distribution of the corporate tax burden as a whole. However, these studies may not indicate who ultimately benefits from deferral and, further, whether deferral is fair and equitable.

The distribution of ultimate beneficiaries, referred to as the economic incidence of the tax benefit, depends on the extent that the tax provision leads to changes in the prices of goods or services. For example, the tax benefit for corporations from deferral may be passed on to consumers through lower prices, to employees through higher wages, or to investors through higher returns. Economic incidence is difficult to determine due to the complexity of the interactions that produce these price and income changes. Studies of the distribution of burdens and benefits usually base their estimates of economic incidence on empirical studies of how prices in relevant markets, including markets for goods and services or labor and capital markets, respond to changes in certain tax provisions. The studies of the corporate tax burden that we identified did not estimate the effect of deferral and their methods may require adjustments before such an estimate can be made. Without these estimates, informed judgments about deferral's fairness will be hard to draw because such judgments depend on knowing who receives the benefit of the tax expenditure. Equally, the distributional effects of the territorial and full inclusion alternatives to deferral are also unknown, and informed judgments about the fairness of the alternatives cannot be made.

Although the ultimate beneficiaries are unknown, there is some evidence that certain industries benefit more from deferral than others. An IRS study found that during the one-time U.S. repatriation tax holiday in 2004, certain industries, such as companies involved in pharmaceutical manufacturing and computer and electronic equipment manufacturing, benefited disproportionately, as they repatriated significantly more income in the form of dividends relative to the size of the tax filers.[37]

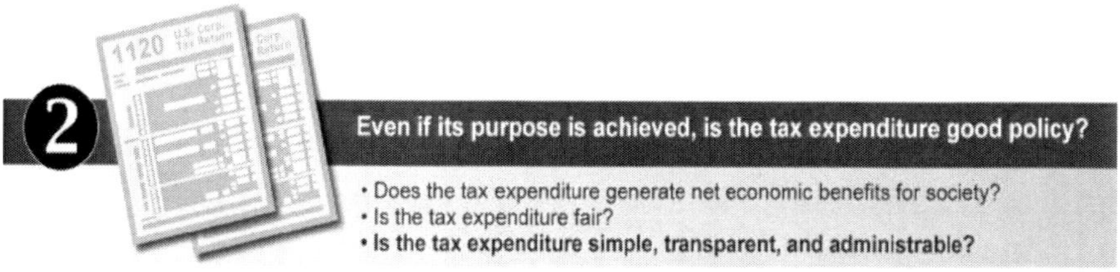

Deferral Adds Complexity to the Tax Code

There is widespread agreement among tax experts that the U.S. system for taxing foreign source income is complex and adds burden for IRS and taxpayers. Deferral contributes to this complex system by enhancing the incentive for corporations to shift income abroad to be taxed at lower rates. Deferral further adds complexity by interacting with a number of tax provisions designed to limit income shifting.[38] One of those provisions, Subpart F of the IRC, creates an exception to the general rule of deferral by defining certain types of passive income, such as interest and royalties, as well as certain other easily manipulated income, as ineligible for deferral. These types of income are viewed as subject to greater manipulation to reduce taxes because they can be artificially shifted between related parties.[39] Moreover, there are also exceptions to Subpart F. As noted previously, interest income that is generated through the primary business activities of financial-services companies of controlled foreign corporations is eligible for deferral. These various provisions add complexity as taxpayers must determine which income can be deferred.

Deferral also affects complexity by interacting with the foreign tax credit and transfer pricing. Our prior work has highlighted these areas as major sources of compliance risk and burden.[40] Deferral allows corporations to time their repatriations of foreign source income for periods when they have excess foreign tax credits, which can be used to lower the amount of U.S. tax they pay. In these cases, complex rules for determining the source of income are required to ensure that the foreign tax credits are applied only against the portion of the corporation's worldwide taxable income attributable to foreign sources.[41] Transfer pricing rules attempt to limit income shifting by requiring that related corporations charge prices for the goods and services they sell to each other that are comparable to market prices. Identifying and evaluating these transfer prices can be difficult for IRS and taxpayers when, as often is the case with intangible property, limited information exists on comparable market prices.

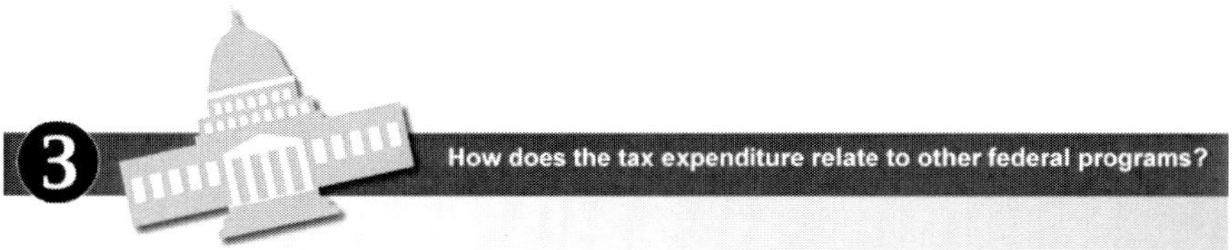

Deferral Does Not Overlap Directly with Other Federal Programs

Our prior work on corporate tax expenditures identified no related federal activities sharing the same reported purpose as the two deferral tax expenditures.[42] Although we have highlighted export promotion programs as an area of potential duplication and overlap, these programs are focused primarily on small companies rather than U.S. multinational corporations.[43] Deferral is integral to the way the United States taxes multinational corporations, and interacts with a number of other tax provisions, such as Subpart F. When considering reform to this system, changes to deferral would need to be coordinated with changes to other tax provisions.

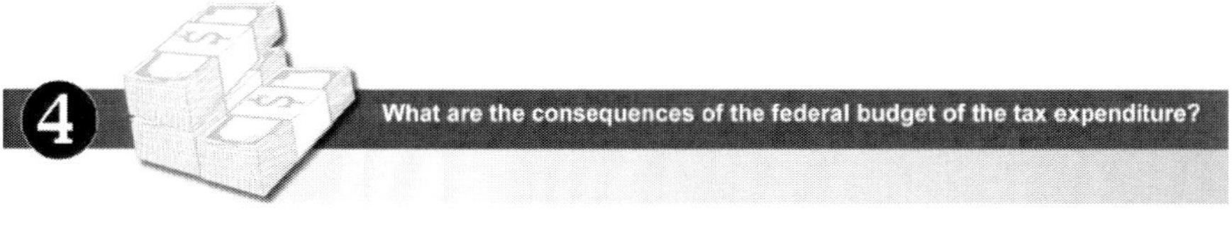

Deferral May Have Relatively Modest Consequences for the Federal Budget but Estimates Vary

According to JCT estimates produced in 2011 and reported by CBO, ending deferral by moving to a full inclusion worldwide system, where foreign source income is taxed whether or not repatriated, would increase federal revenues by $4.7 billion in 2012. According to the same estimates, exempting active foreign dividends from U.S. tax, similar to that of a territorial tax system, and changing the tax treatment of overhead expenses would increase revenues by $3.3 billion in 2012.[44]

These estimates are based on specific proposals to change the tax code, and include behavioral responses by taxpayers to the tax change.[45] The revenue estimate for exempting active foreign dividends shows an increase in revenue chiefly because the expense allocation rules under this option reduced the expenses that can be deducted from U.S. income relative to the current system's expense allocation rules.[46]

The effect on U.S. tax revenue of full inclusion and territoriality depends on the incentives the alternatives provide to shift income out of the United States and its taxing authority and the specifics of the alternatives' design. The incentive to locate income in low-tax countries may be less under full inclusion and higher under the territorial system, thereby eroding the U.S. corporate tax base.[47] However, territorial systems in practice include design features, such as a minimum tax on foreign source income, that are intended to limit these losses.

JCT and Treasury also make tax expenditure estimates on a regular basis that do not account for how taxpayer behavior may change when a tax expenditure is altered. Although these estimates do not represent the amount of revenue that would be gained if deferral were eliminated, they can indicate how revenue losses may be changing over time. The tax expenditure estimates show that revenue losses from the general deferral tax expenditure have increased significantly.[48] These estimates of increasing tax revenue losses are consistent with changes in the location of earnings of U.S. corporations. During this period, U.S. corporations were earning an increasing share of their profits from foreign sources, likely increasing the amount of income deferred abroad. As seen in figure 2, U.S. corporate profits earned abroad, compared to total U.S. corporate profits, have increased moderately since 1997.

Source: GAO analysis of Bureau of Economic Analysis data.

Figure 2. Ratio of U.S. Corporate Profits Earned Abroad to Total U.S. Corporate Profits, 1987-2012.

In addition, a number of legislative changes may have affected the revenue losses from deferral by making it easier to shift or keep income abroad. These include the look-through rule exception from Subpart F. This rule provides that dividends, interest, rents, and royalties received or accrued by one controlled foreign corporation from a related controlled foreign corporation are not treated as Subpart F income, and are eligible for deferral.[49] Finally, some have suggested that in light of the U.S. tax repatriation holiday in 2004, which allowed U.S. corporations to exempt most dividends from tax on a one-time basis, U.S. multinational corporations may have accumulated foreign earnings abroad in anticipation of another repatriation holiday.[50]

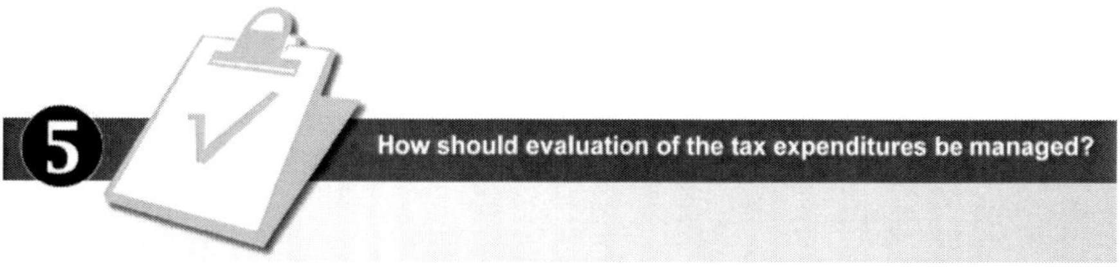

No Consensus Exists on Which Agency Should Evaluate Deferral

No federal agency has been tasked to evaluate deferral. Since 1994, we have recommended greater scrutiny of tax expenditures, as periodic reviews could help determine how well specific tax expenditures work to achieve their goals, and how their benefits and costs compare to those of programs with similar goals.[51] However, as we reported in June 2013, the Office of Management and Budget (OMB) has not developed a framework for reviewing tax expenditure performance.[52] We made a number of recommendations to OMB, including that it provide guidance to agencies to identify tax expenditures that contribute to each appropriate agency goal. In July 2013, OMB released guidance that directs agencies to identify tax expenditures that contribute to their goals.[53]

EVALUATION OF GRADUATED CORPORATE INCOME TAX RATE SCHEDULE

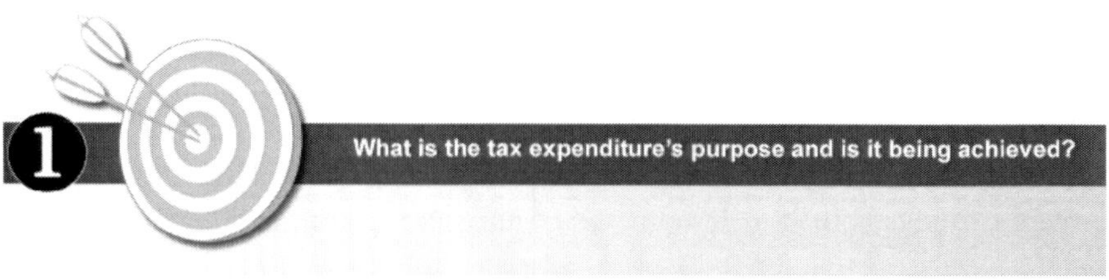

The Graduated Corporate Income Tax Rate Schedule's Purpose Is Viewed as Supporting Small Businesses, but It May Not Be Well Targeted to That Purpose

The purpose of the graduated corporate income tax rate schedule has generally been described in the academic literature and by tax experts as supporting small businesses by reducing their tax burden. The tax expenditure benefits businesses that organize under Subchapter C of the IRC, "C corporations," by taxing their income at reduced tax rates when the income falls beneath certain limits. To the extent that small corporations have income beneath these limits, they could benefit from the reduced rates.[54]

Some rationales for providing this tax benefit to smaller businesses include encouraging entrepreneurship, innovation, and small business growth and employment. It has been argued in some academic literature that the greater after-tax income may make the small businesses more attractive to investors, and may alleviate a lack of access to capital that small businesses experience due to limited information on their business model or profit potential. Similar justifications have been made for providing benefits through other federal programs, such as federal small business loan programs. CRS' tax expenditure compendium details how the graduated corporate income tax rate schedule has developed and changed legislatively over time.[55]

Evidence is mixed on whether the lower corporate tax rates provided by the graduated rate schedule increases business formation.[56] Some research shows that, although only a small number of start-up companies initially form as C corporations, when and if these businesses generate profits, they have an incentive to incorporate so that these profits are taxed at lower corporate tax rates. However, other research has also indicated that incentives can produce the opposite effect. Businesses are less likely to incorporate if corporate tax rates are high, compared to individual tax rates, and instead may choose another form of business entity that is taxed under the individual tax rates.[57] In contrast, businesses with losses will typically prefer not to incorporate so that these losses can be deducted from other higher taxed personal income. Research has also shown that in 2007 a majority of unincorporated small businesses faced a marginal tax rate of 10 to 25 percent, making the rates they paid comparable to those of the graduated corporate income tax rates.[58] IRS data have also shown that the number of businesses that organize themselves as C corporations has declined, while those organizing as S corporations and partnerships have been rising in the past decade. See figure 3.

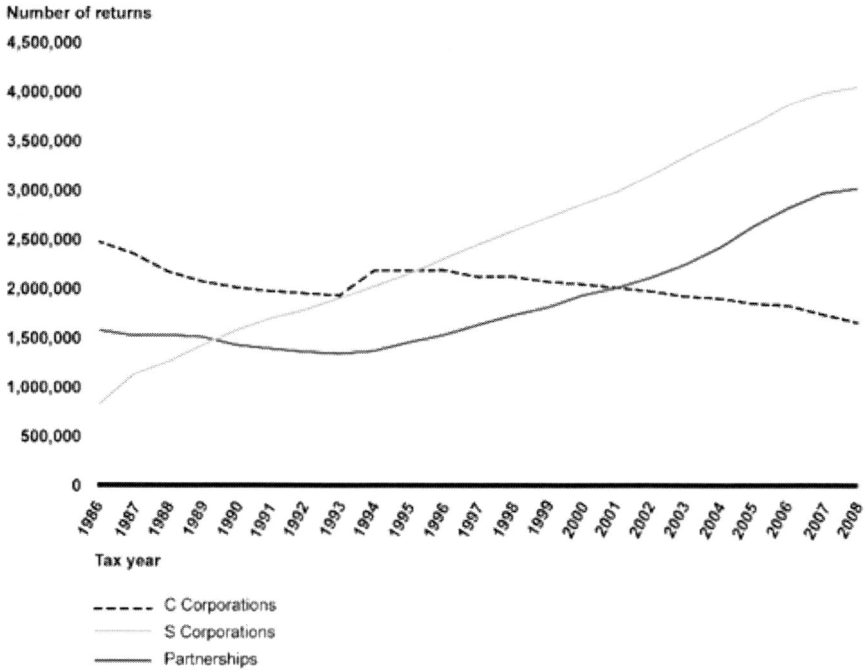

Source: GAO analysis of IRS data.

Figure 3. Number of Returns by Form of Business, Tax Year 1986-2008.

Evidence from aggregated corporate tax return data suggests that the graduated corporate income tax rate schedule may not be well targeted at supporting small businesses. As table 2 indicates, some corporations that may not be considered small businesses claimed one of the graduated rates and received the tax benefit. For example, as table 2 shows, about 23 percent of corporations with positive taxable income that had business receipts from between $10 million and $50 million had less than $75,000 in taxable income, and benefited from the two lowest graduated rates.[59] The use of taxable income as an indicator of the size of a business may include businesses that are large by other indicators, such as total assets.

Neither Treasury nor IRS has established performance measures for the graduated corporate income tax rate schedule to measure its effect, and whether it is achieving its purpose. As we previously found, most agencies have not focused on identifying the contributions tax expenditures make towards agency goals.[60]

Table 2. Percentage of Corporations with Positive Taxable Income by Taxable Income and Size of Business Receipts, 2010

		Corporate income tax rate bracket		
Size of business receipts	First $50,000 (15 percent)	$50,000 - $75,000 (25 percent)	$75,000 - $100,000 (34 percent)	Over $100,000 (34 percent or more)
Under $25,000	90.5%	3.3%	1.3%	4.9%
$25,000 under $100,000	95.3%	3.3%	0.6%	0.9%
$100,000 under $250,000	89.4%	5.6%	2.6%	2.4%
$250,000 under $500,000	83.6%	6.5%	5.0%	4.9%
$500,000 under $1,000,000	79.5%	10.0%	3.2%	7.2%
$1,000,000 under $2,500,000	68.8%	12.2%	5.9%	13.1%
$2,500,000 under $5,000,000	52.4%	13.0%	6.7%	28.0%
$5,000,000 under $10,000,000	31.0%	13.1%	7.6%	48.2%
$10,000,000 under $50,000,000	16.3%	6.2%	5.2%	72.4%
$50,000,000 under $100,000,000	4.4%	1.7%	2.2%	91.8%
$100,000,000 under $250,000,000	0.9%	0.9%	0.7%	97.5%
$250,000,000 and over	0.2%	0.2%	0.0%	99.7%

Source: GAO analysis of Internal Revenue Service Statistics of Income Corporate Tax File Data estimates, tax year 2010.

Notes: Data on the number of corporations are from IRS SOI corporate file and include active corporations that filed a return on forms 1120, 1120-F, 1120-L, and 1120-PC, but not forms 1120S, 1120-REIT, and 1120-RIC. The coefficient of variation for the estimates can be found in table 4, see appendix III.

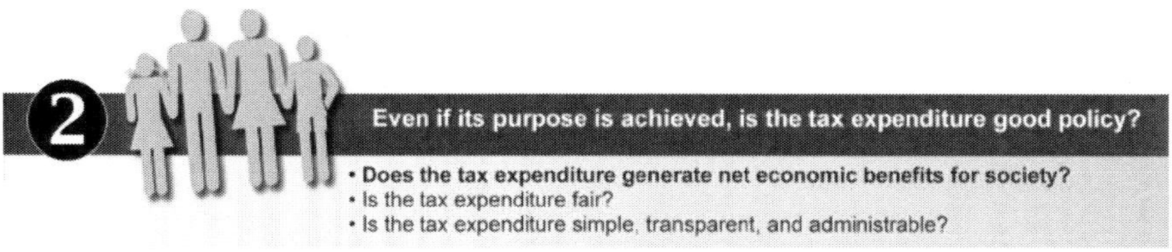

Efficiency Effects of the Graduated Rates Are Disputed

Some academic literature has suggested that the graduated rates can cause inefficiency by providing relief to some corporations and not others depending on their taxable income. The economy is less efficient if the rates divert resources from one type of corporation to another based on tax considerations, rather than how productively the corporations use the resources. Other sources of potential inefficiency include the incentive provided by the graduated rates for small businesses to form as C corporations to take advantage of lower corporate rates, compared to those of individual tax rates. A Treasury study found that higher differentials between corporate and non-corporate tax rates increased the likelihood that a firm will convert from C to S corporation status after the Tax Reform Act of 1986.[61] In this case, small businesses may choose an organizational form that they would not have selected without the tax incentive, suggesting that this may not be the most productive way for them to organize their operations.[62]

The graduated rates could be justified on efficiency grounds if, from society's point of view, without the incentive too few small businesses are formed given their potential for profit and innovation. It has been argued by some research that small businesses need support because they provide a disproportionate share of innovation and net job creation. However, more recent research has shown that a small number of new businesses may generate most of the innovation and net job creation. If this is the case, targeted federal support for certain small businesses may be more effective than graduated rates that apply to all corporations with less than a certain amount taxable income.[63]

The magnitude of the efficiency effects of the graduated rates has not been estimated, but experts agree that the effect of reducing or eliminating the rates will depend on how the change is implemented. For example, reducing or eliminating the rates without making similar changes to individual tax rates may motivate companies to change organizational form—from C corporations to "pass-through" entities like S corporations and partnerships—to take advantage of the differences between corporate and individual income tax rates.

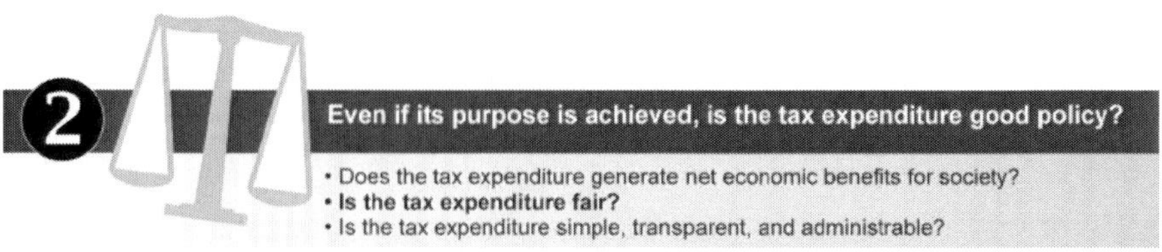

Informed Judgments about the Graduated Rates' Equity Require Information about Ultimate Beneficiaries

As with the deferral tax expenditures, studies that specifically estimate the distribution of the benefits from the graduated corporate income tax rate schedule are unavailable. Without these estimates, conclusions about the fairness of the tax expenditures will be hard to draw because such judgments depend on who bears the burden of the tax or receives the benefit of the tax expenditure. The ultimate beneficiaries depend on the extent that the tax provision leads people to make decisions that change the prices of goods or services. Just as in the case of the deferral tax benefit, the benefit of graduated rates may be passed on to consumers through lower prices, employees through higher wages, or to investors through higher returns.[64]

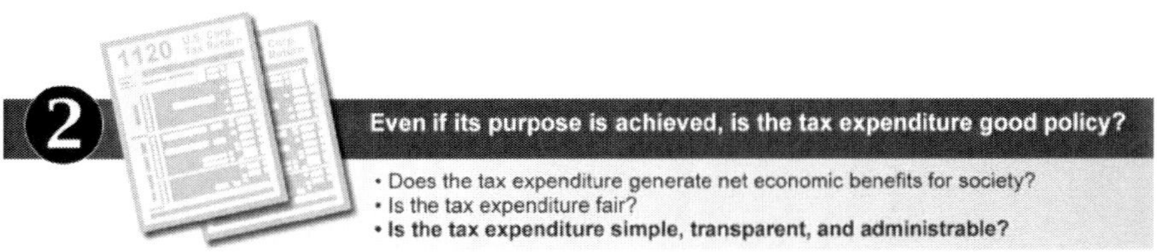

The Graduated Rates Likely Add Little Complexity to Determing Tax Liability But Some Evidence of Tax Planning Has Been Found

Although we did not find any estimates that isolate the compliance and administrative costs associated with the graduated rates, both costs are likely to be relatively low. IRS officials could not highlight any administrative or compliance issues involved with administering the graduated corporate income tax rate schedule. They said that applying the graduated corporate income rate schedule for a particular taxpayer is primarily a computational issue, and does not present much uncertainty to taxpayers in determining their tax liabilities. However, IRS research has found some evidence that corporations' taxable income tends to cluster below rate changes introduced by the tax rate brackets. The research found that if the tax net income of corporations in their sample of Schedule M-3 filers (generally those with assets of at least $10 million) from tax years 2004 through 2008 rose 5 percent, a substantial number of corporations would face higher marginal tax rates.[65] This clustering of filers around certain tax rates may be the result of tax planning that increases compliance costs.

The compliance and administrative costs of the graduated rates have not been estimated separately from the costs of complying with and administering all the provisions of the corporate income tax. However, estimates of the total compliance burden of small businesses may give some context to the compliance costs associated with graduated rates. A 2007 study of businesses with assets of less than $10 million in 2002 found that small businesses initially face significant fixed compliance costs, which increase at a decreasing rate as the business grows.[66] However, the specific administrative and compliance costs of the graduated rates may not be a large part of these costs compared with other, more complicated provisions of the tax code.

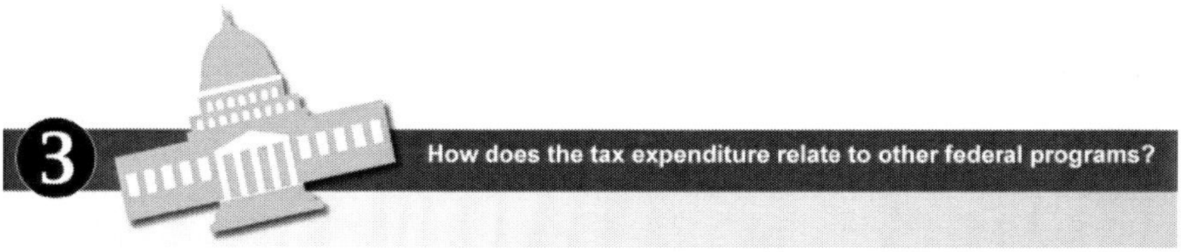

Graduated Rates Are Related to a Number of Spending Programs but the Relative Effectiveness of the Tax Expenditure Has Not Been Assessed

Our prior work on corporate tax expenditures found no related federal spending program sharing the same reported purpose as the graduated rates of supporting small businesses that adopt the corporate form of legal organization.[67] However, there are federal spending programs that share, at least in part, the similar purpose of supporting entrepreneurs and small businesses. In prior work, we identified 52 programs at the U.S. Departments of Agriculture, Commerce, and Housing and Urban Development, and the Small Business Administration, which all overlap with at least one other program in terms of the type of assistance they are authorized to offer, and the type of entrepreneur they are authorized to serve.[68]

Changes in the graduated rates are generally part of proposals to reduce the overall corporate tax rate which are discussed in the context of tax reform. The issue of whether the tax expenditure could be better designed to target small business or spending or non-tax policies that support small businesses may be preferable but has not been part of the discussion.

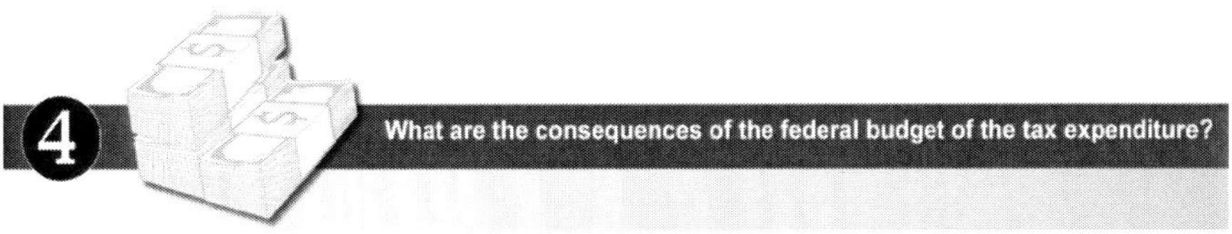

Moving to a Flat Corporate Income Tax Rate of 35 Percent Would Have Relatively Modest Consequences for the Federal Budget

According to JCT estimates produced in 2011 and reported by CBO, moving to a single corporate rate of 35 percent would have raised $1.5 billion in 2012.[69]

This estimate is based on a specific proposal to change the tax code, and includes behavioral responses by taxpayers to the tax change. JCT and Treasury also annually calculate tax expenditure estimates that do not account for how taxpayer behavior may change when a tax expenditure is altered. Because they do not account for these behavioral changes or interactions with other tax provisions, the tax expenditure estimates available for the graduated rates do not represent the amount of revenue that would be gained if these rates were repealed.

However, as mentioned above in the case of deferral, these estimates can indicate how revenue losses may be changing over time. As shown in figure 4, estimated tax revenue losses from the graduated corporate income tax rate schedule have decreased in the past decade. From 1998 through 2012, estimated tax revenue losses fell from $7.3 billion to $4.3 billion in constant 2012 dollars.

The estimated fiscal year 2012 loss was 3 percent of all estimated revenue losses from corporate tax expenditures ($147 billion). The estimate was equal to 1.8 percent of corporate tax revenue in 2012. The decrease in figure 4 may be due, in part, to less companies incorporating as C corporations, which we highlighted above.

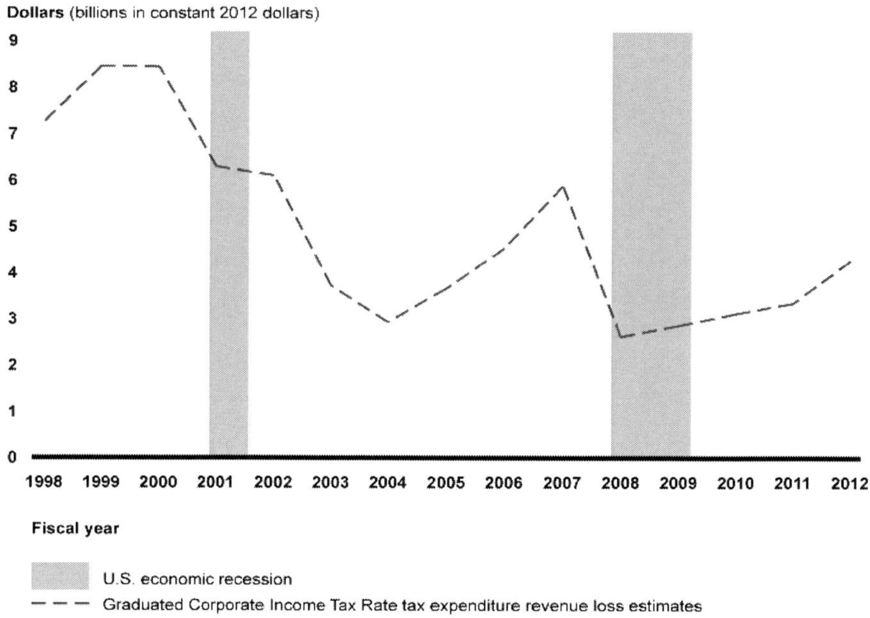

Source: GAO analysis of OMB budget, fiscal years 2000-2014.

Figure 4. Estimated Federal Tax Revenue Losses Due to Graduated Corporate Income Tax Rate Schedule, Reported by Treasury, 1998-2012.

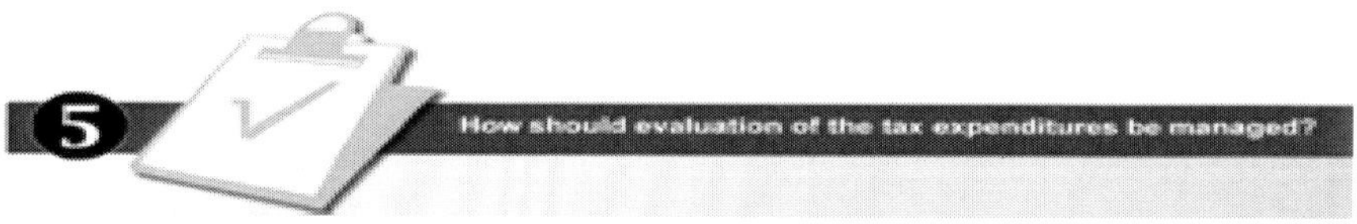

No Consensus Exists on Which Agency Should Evaluate the Graduated Corporate Tax Rate Schedule

As in the case of the deferral tax expenditures, no agency has been tasked with evaluating the graduated corporate income tax rate schedule. In June 2013, we made a number of recommendations to OMB, including that it should provide guidance to agencies to identify tax expenditures that contribute to each appropriate agency goal.[70] In July 2013, OMB released guidance that directs agencies to identify tax expenditures that contribute to their goals.[71]

AGENCY AND THIRD PARTY COMMENTS AND OUR EVALUATION

We provided a draft of this report to the Secretary of the Treasury and the Commissioner of Internal Revenue for comment. We also asked the Joint Committee on Taxation (JCT) and all external experts we interviewed to review a draft of this report. Treasury, IRS, JCT, and external experts provided technical comments that were incorporated, as appropriate.

James R. White
Director,
Tax Issues Strategic Issues

APPENDIX I: OBJECTIVES, SCOPE, AND METHODOLOGY

This report uses our tax expenditures evaluation guide to determine what is known about following three tax expenditures: (1) the deferral of income for controlled foreign corporations; (2) deferred taxes for certain financial firms on income earned overseas; and (3) the graduated corporate income tax rate. Because deferred taxes for certain financial firms on income earned overseas is a special case of the treatment of foreign source income of all controlled foreign corporations, our first section of the report focuses our discussion on the more general case of all controlled foreign corporations using deferral. Our second section of the report covers the graduated corporate income tax rate schedule. For both sections of the report, we cover the five questions outlined in our guide and listed below to determine what is known about each tax expenditure. We highlight what questions we are answering for each tax expenditure at the beginning of each section of the report.

GAO Tax Expenditure Evaluation Guide

To evaluate the three tax expenditures above, we applied our tax expenditure evaluation guide, which was issued in November 2012.[1] The guide outlines a series of questions and sub-questions that can be used to evaluate tax expenditures. The five primary questions and sub-questions outlined in the guide are:

1. What is the tax expenditure's purpose and is being achieved?
   - What is the tax expenditure's intended purpose?
   - Have performance measures been established to monitor success in achieving the tax expenditure's intended purpose?
   - Does the tax expenditure succeed in achieving its intended purpose?
2. Even if its purpose is achieved, is the tax expenditure good policy?
   - Does the tax expenditure generate net economic benefits for society?
   - Is the tax expenditure fair?
   - Is the tax expenditure simple, transparent, and administrable?
3. How does the tax expenditure relate to other federal programs?
   - Does the tax expenditure contribute to a designated cross-agency priority goal?
   - Does the tax expenditure duplicate or overlap with another federal effort?
   - Is the tax expenditure being coordinated with other federal activities?
   - Would an alternative to the tax expenditure more effectively achieve its intended purpose?
4. What are the consequences for the federal budget of the tax expenditure?
   - Are there budget effects not captured by Treasury's or the Joint Committee on Taxation's tax expenditure estimates?
   - Are there options for limiting the tax expenditure's revenue loss?
5. How should evaluation of the tax expenditure be managed?
   - What agency or agencies should evaluate the tax expenditure?
   - When should the tax expenditure be evaluated?
   - What data are needed to evaluate the tax expenditure?

The guide's questions cover a number of different policy objectives. Sometimes, these objectives compete. This report provides information responsive to the questions, but does not attempt to balance the different objectives or make recommendations. Rather, policymakers are better positioned to judge how competing policy objectives should be weighed. As we note in our tax expenditure evaluation guide, it is not a "one size fits all" framework for evaluating tax expenditures. We used reasonable judgment in applying the guide's questions and concepts to evaluate the three tax expenditures. In some instances, we focused our discussion on certain questions in the guide because they were more relevant to the tax expenditures we were evaluating, while devoting less discussion to others that were more technical in nature.

- Question 1 above covers the tax expenditure's intended purpose and if it is being achieved. Since the purpose of the deferral tax expenditures is unclear, we did not address the sub-questions related to whether the deferral tax expenditures achieve their intended purpose, and if performance measures have been established.
- For question 2 above, our discussion of the deferral tax expenditures and criteria for good policy also includes question 3 above which covers alternatives to the tax expenditures, as there is a natural relation to alternative proposals and how they may affect the criteria outlined in question 2.

To the extent that we use our tax expenditure evaluation guide in the future on other tax expenditures, the structure and focus of future reports may differ from how it is presented in this report. To determine what is known about the deferral tax expenditures and the graduated corporate income tax rate schedule by answering the five questions listed above, we reviewed the following sources:

- Our previous work on tax expenditures, tax reform, tax policy and administration, duplication, overlap, and fragmentation, and results-oriented government and program evaluation.
- Previous work by the Congressional Research Service (CRS), the Congressional Budget Office (CBO), the Joint Committee on Taxation (JCT), the Department of the Treasury (Treasury), and the Internal Revenue Service (IRS).
- Legislation, statutes, and regulations.
- Academic and scholarly research on the tax expenditures and corporate taxation. To identify academic literature, we searched terms and certain authors in a number of academic literature databases, such as ProQuest, Econlit, and Social SciSearch. We reviewed and identified academic literature cited in CRS' tax expenditure compendium, and a comprehensive study by JCT on foreign direct investment.[2] We reviewed articles published in the National Tax Journal and asked Treasury, IRS, and the external experts we interviewed for recommendations on articles to review. We also

interviewed Treasury and IRS officials, and external experts affiliated with CRS and two universities, who specialize in the U.S. corporate income tax system. The results from these interviews are not generalizable.

- Treasury tax expenditure estimates for fiscal years 1998 through 2012, and estimates by JCT on the revenue effects of making changes to the tax expenditures in our scope.[3] To identify how the deferral and graduated corporate income tax rate schedule tax expenditures have changed in terms of their aggregate estimated revenue losses, we analyzed tax expenditure estimates developed by the Treasury and reported by the Office of Management and Budget in the Federal Budget's Analytical Perspectives for fiscal years 1998 through 2012.[4] We converted all tax expenditure estimates for each fiscal year into 2012 constant dollars to adjust for inflation. We did so by using the chain price indexes reported in the fiscal year 2014 federal budget. While sufficiently reliable as a gauge of general magnitude, summing tax expenditure estimates do not take into account any interactions between tax expenditures. In addition, tax expenditure estimates do not incorporate any behavioral responses. Thus, they do not represent the revenue amount that would be gained if a specific tax expenditure was repealed. To identify JCT estimates of the revenue effects of making changes to the tax expenditures in our scope, we reviewed CBO's latest report that outlines spending and revenue options. These options outline a number of changes to the tax expenditures in our scope with accompanying estimates from JCT.[5] Its revenue-effect estimates take into account a number of behavioral changes, unlike the tax expenditure estimates that Treasury and JCT complete. These include possible behavioral changes in: (1) corporate dividends and retained earnings; (2) the corporate capital structure; (3) corporate equity valuations; (4) repatriations of deferred foreign income; and (5) business entity choice.[6]
- Data estimates from IRS Statistics of Income (SOI) Corporate Tax File, 2010, the most recent year available at the time of our work, and Bureau of Economic Analysis (BEA) data on corporate profits from 1987 through 2012. We requested estimates from the IRS SOI 2010 Corporate Tax File on the number of C corporations by their corporate income tax bracket, and a measurement of their size—in this case—business receipts. Data compiled by IRS SOI are based on a stratified random sample of 63,630 corporate income tax returns for 2010 from

corporations that end their corporate year from July 1, 2010, through June 30, 2011. These estimates are subject to sampling errors. The margin of error is based on a 95-percent confidence interval. For our report, IRS SOI provided data on C corporations, which include active corporations filing tax forms 1120, 1120-F, 1120-L, and 1120-PC. Data are not included for "pass-through" entities, which file on forms 1120S, 1120-REIT, and 1120-RIC. We used business receipts as our measurement of size and used IRS' breakout for the different sizes of business receipts. We also obtained data from IRS on the number of different types of business form entities (C corporations, S corporations, and partnerships) from 1986 to 2008. We also analyzed data from BEA on corporate profits by industry from 1987 to 2012. To determine how the composition of U.S. corporate profits have changed over time, we took a ratio of the amount of profit earned by U.S. corporations abroad compared to the total amount of profits earned by U.S. corporations. This analysis was based on a similar analysis used in academic literature.[7]

To assess the reliability of the data and estimates, we reviewed agency documentation, interviewed agency officials, and reviewed our prior reports that have used the data and estimates. We determined that Treasury, JCT, BEA, and IRS data and estimates were sufficiently reliable for our purposes. However, the IRS SOI corporate sample may not provide a precise estimate of the number of taxpayers claiming a tax expenditure when the number of taxpayers is very small. We conducted our work from April to September 2013 in accordance with all sections of GAO's Quality Assurance Framework that are relevant to our objectives. The framework requires that we plan and perform the engagement to obtain sufficient and appropriate evidence to meet our stated objectives, and to discuss any limitations in our work. We believe that the information and data obtained and the analysis conducted provide a reasonable basis for any findings and conclusions in this product.

APPENDIX II: COMPARISON OF TERRITORIAL AND WORLDWIDE CORPORATE INCOME TAX SYSTEMS

Many proposals for changing the way the current U.S. system taxes foreign source income are detailed and complex.[1] In general, however, they involve redesigning the current system to more resemble a pure worldwide or a pure territorial system. The basic designs of the three systems being considered as alternatives are the following:

- The current worldwide system with deferral. Foreign active business income is taxed when repatriated as dividends to the U.S. This system has a foreign tax credit limited to the U.S. tax liability on foreign source income, and certain anti-deferral provisions like Subpart F.
- A territorial system that uses a dividend exemption. The dividends derived from foreign active business income can be repatriated without U.S. tax. This system would continue to tax Subpart F income as do most countries with territorial systems.
- A worldwide system with full inclusion. The current worldwide system is retained, but deferral of foreign active business income is eliminated.

The current system serves as a benchmark against which to compare the alternatives. When applying the criteria of a good tax system, the territorial and worldwide systems with full inclusion are examined for their effect on efficiency, equity, and complexity, and their relativity to the effects of the current system. Figure 5 illustrates how the basic design of the full inclusion worldwide system and the territorial system affects the taxes that corporations pay.

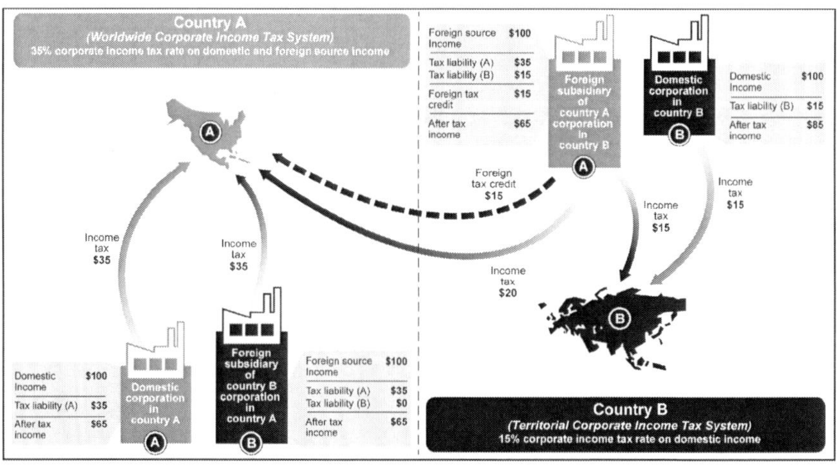

Source: GAO analysis.

Figure 5. Example of Worldwide and Territorial Corporate Income Tax Systems.

As shown in figure 5, Country A has a worldwide tax system that taxes income of its domestic corporations, and that of foreign corporations earned within its borders at the same 35-percent rate.

The domestic corporation and the subsidiary of the foreign corporation each pay $35 in taxes to Country A. Additionally, Country A taxes the income of the foreign subsidiaries of its corporations at the same 35-percent rate. However, in this case, it provides a credit for taxes paid to the country in which the subsidiary operates.

The subsidiary gets a $15 credit for the tax it pays to Country B, and subtracts this amount from the $35 tax liability that it owes its home Country A.

The total tax paid by the subsidiary is $15 to Country B plus the $20 net tax that it pays at home for an overall tax of $35. For the worldwide system, taxes paid are the same for corporations operating within Country A, and for its corporations operating abroad.

In a territorial system, income is taxed only by the country in which it is earned. In figure 5, Country B has a territorial system that imposes a 15-percent tax on corporations that operate within its borders. The domestic corporation and the subsidiary of the foreign corporation remit the same tax payment of $15 to Country B on $100 of income earned there. Unlike the worldwide system, the territorial system imposes no tax on the income of the foreign subsidiaries of its own corporations. For the territorial system, taxes paid are equal for corporations operating within Country B, but differ for corporations operating across borders.

As discussed above, the experts we interviewed agreed and economic theory suggests that any corporate tax system's overall effect on efficiency depends on its relative effect on different types of investment decisions. The full inclusion system is likely to increase investment location efficiency relative to the current and territorial systems. Under the current system, investment abroad has a lower tax cost when repatriation of the foreign source income is deferred.

Full inclusion would eliminate this tax advantage, and would be more consistent with efficient location decisions. When the foreign tax rate is lower than the U.S. tax rate, domestic corporations under full inclusion pay taxes on income earned at home and abroad at the same rate—the U.S. tax rate. The system does not provide incentives either to invest abroad or at home (i.e. it is neutral with respect to the location of investment).[2]

The territorial system, on the other hand, may increase investment location inefficiencies by making the location incentives that arise when countries adopt different tax rates permanent.

However, as previously noted in this report, these inefficiencies may be offset to some extent by improved ownership efficiencies and reduced incentives to move corporate residences abroad. Corporations operating under a territorial system pay the same tax rate on income from their operations in each country.

This would eliminate any tax advantage that would allow a less efficient owner in that country to acquire the more productive corporation. While the full inclusion system may not distort location decisions, it may distort decisions about who owns the foreign subsidiaries. Some advocates of the territorial system argue that efficiency gains from eliminating this ownership distortion can offset any efficiency losses from distorted location decisions.

The experts whom we interviewed and the research that we reviewed agreed that both the territorial and full inclusion systems eliminate efficiency cost from the lockout effect that exists under the current system. Full inclusion eliminates the lockout effect by making foreign-earned income taxable without repatriation.

The territorial system eliminates the lockout effect by making foreign-earned income tax free, whether or not they are repatriated. The effect of the lockout's elimination could be significant because of possibly large efficiency costs due to growing accumulations of income abroad.

Some research has suggested that income-shifting incentives should be significantly reduced under full inclusion, but may be increased under the territorial system. Researchers have found evidence of extensive income shifting under the current system.[3] Full inclusion nearly eliminates incentives for income shifting because corporations pay the same rate under full inclusion, regardless of where the income is located and the timing of its repatriation.[4] The territorial system, on the other hand, would likely increase the incentive to shift income to lower-tax countries because income earned abroad would be exempt from being taxed, even when repatriated.

The relative effects of the alternatives on compliance and administrative burden depend on the specifics of their design. As described above, the current system is complex, and imposes compliance and administrative burden by requiring extensive calculations and adjustments involving foreign tax credits, sourcing rules for income and expenses, and transfer-pricing rules to limit income shifting.

Some research has shown that, while a full inclusion system would reduce the benefits and scope for income shifting, it would also retain some of the current system's burden, such as the foreign tax credit and sourcing rules for income and expenses.

The territorial system, by increasing income-shifting incentives, may require provisions to protect the tax base that can add considerable complexity to the tax code. The degree of complexity relative to the current system will depend in part on how much of the current rules are maintained or expanded in the new system.

However, because both the territorial and full inclusion systems remove any incentive to delay repatriation, they would eliminate compliance and administrative burden due to the repatriation tax planning that occurs under the current system.

Based on the research and revenue estimates we reviewed, the revenue raised by each system depends on the specifics of its design. How much of the potential worldwide tax revenue a country gets depends on its tax system's incentives to relocate income to a lower tax rate country. Some research has noted that under full inclusion, the corporation has no incentive to relocate income to a lower tax country unless it has excess foreign tax credits.

However, under a territorial tax system, the corporation has an incentive to move income to a lower tax rate foreign country. Based on these incentives, it would appear that revenue for the home country is likely to decrease when a country moves from a worldwide to a territorial system. However, the relative effects on revenue ultimately depend on the details of the design. For example, some features of a territorial system's design are implemented specifically to limit revenue losses.

Under its territorial system, Japan imposes a per-country minimum tax, which means that corporations will lack incentives to locate income in a country with a tax rate below the minimum.[5] Other features of a tax system that affect revenues include changes in income and expense allocation rules that would increase foreign source income attributed to the home country under a territorial system.

Appendix III: IRS Statistics of Income Data on the Number of C Corporations by Taxable Income and Size of Business Receipts, 2010

Table 3. Number of Corporate Taxpayers by Taxable Income and Size of Business Receipts, 2010

Size of business receipts	No taxable income	First $50,000 (15 percent)	$50,000 - $75,000 (25 percent)	$75,000 - $100,000 (34 percent)	$100,000 - $335,000 (39 percent)	$335,000 - $10,000,000 (34 percent)	$10,000,000 $15,000,000 (35 percent)	$15,000,000 $18,333,333 (38 percent)	Over $18,333,333 (35 percent)
Under $25,000	353,943	67,381	2,427	996	2,471	1,107	14	11	43
$25,000 under $100,000	181,917	65,036	2,251	383	440	166	**	**	3
$100,000 under $250,000	183,569	68,107	4,304	1,945	1,753	83	**	**	**
$250,000 under $500,000	137,421	51,575	3,980	3,071	2,702	340	**	**	**
$500,000 under $1,000,000	116,640	48,000	6,043	1,948	3,804	560	3	**	0
$1,000,000 under $2,500,000	101,849	46,875	8,325	4,014	6,868	2,027	6	**	3
$2,500,000 under $5,000,000	43,176	18,972	4,701	2,416	6,749	3,369	4	**	6
$5,000,000 under $10,000,000	21,690	7,560	3,204	1,860	6,772	4,955	9	3	10
$10,000,000 under $50,000,000	19,801	4,014	1,531	1,280	6,112	11,455	152	56	98
$50,000,000 under $100,000,000	2,934	167	63	86	479	2,649	190	50	150

Size of business receipts	No taxable income	First $50,000 (15 percent)	$50,000 - $75,000 (25 percent)	$75,000 - $100,000 (34 percent)	$100,000 - $335,000 (39 percent)	$335,000 - $10,000,000 (34 percent)	$10,000,000 $15,000,000 (35 percent)	$15,000,000 $18,333,333 (38 percent)	Over $18,333,333 (35 percent)
$100,000,000 under $250,000,000	2,081	24	23	19	127	1,564	292	135	457
$250,000,000 and over	2,140	5	5	0	26	662	235	111	2,112

Source: IRS Statistics of Income (SOI) Corporate Tax File data estimates, tax year 2010.

Note: Data on the number of corporations are from IRS SOI Corporate Tax File, and include active corporations that filed a return on forms 1120, 1120-F, 1120-L, and 1120-PC, but not forms 1120S, 1120-REIT, and 1120-RIC.

** Data have been combined with data in a lower size class to avoid disclosure for specific corporations.

Table 4. Coefficient of Variation Calculations for Totals in Table 3

Size of Business Receipts	No taxable income	First $50,000 (15 percent)	$50,000 - $75,000 25 percent)	$75,000 - $100,000 (34 percent)	$100,000 - $335,000 (39 percent)	$335,000 - $10,000,000 (34 percent)	$10,000,000- $15,000,000 (35 percent)	$15,000,000- $18,333,333 (38 percent)	Over $18,333,333 (35 percent)	Row Total
Under $25,000	4.28	10.70	57.40	89.45	56.67	81.84	205.37	733.58	16.50	3.80
$25,000 under $100,000	6.31	10.90	59.55	139.22	132.98	211.65	—	—	51.64	5.27
$100,000 under $250,000	6.27	10.65	43.08	64.04	67.05	291.45	—	—	—	5.15
$250,000 under $500,000	7.35	12.28	44.76	51.01	54.03	150.34	—	—	—	5.99

Table 4. (Continued)

Size of Business Receipts	No taxable income	First $50,000 (15 percent)	$50,000 - $75,000 25 percent)	$75,000 - $100,000 (34 percent)	$100,000 - $335,000 (39 percent)	$335,000 - $10,000,000 (34 percent)	$10,000,000- $15,000,000 (35 percent)	$15,000,000- $18,333,333 (38 percent)	Over $18,333,333 (35 percent)	Row Total
$500,000 under $1,000,000	8.02	12.74	36.32	63.94	45.62	115.06	—	—	—	6.39
$1,000,000 under $2,500,000	8.60	12.89	30.84	44.47	33.87	61.07	0.00	—	51.64	6.53
$2,500,000 under $5,000,000	13.32	20.38	41.05	57.13	33.90	45.50	0.00	—	44.70	9.73
$5,000,000 under $10,000,000	18.60	32.31	49.65	65.15	33.87	36.80	53.95	89.27	34.62	12.71
$10,000,000 under $50,000,000	18.46	44.14	71.52	77.80	35.50	23.86	10.89	17.40	12.33	12.39
$50,000,000 under $100,000,000	36.36	206.26	329.60	302.03	123.58	44.41	9.75	16.27	8.9	26.00
$100,000,000 under $250,000,000	25.48	487.74	478.36	580.59	210.34	40.56	165.20	23.53	17.78	21.51
$250,000,000 and over	4.81	798.88	798.50	—	460.64	30.59	6.64	8.03	0.88	5.00

Source: GAO analysis of IRS Statistics of Income (SOI) Corporate Tax File data estimates, tax year 2010.

Note: This table contains the coefficient of variation. It is the estimate divided by the standard error. The estimate can be either a total or a percent. When the estimate is small (1 percent or 5 corporations), the coefficient of variation may be more than 100. Data on the number of corporations are from IRS SOI Corporate Tax File, and include active corporations that filed a return on forms 1120, 1120-F, 1120-L, and 1120-PC, but not forms 1120S, 1120-REIT, and 1120-RIC.

— The sample has no observations in this cell. The population may have corporations in this cell. However, we do not have sufficient information to calculate an appropriate margin of error.

End Notes

[1] Our prior work highlighted a number of tax expenditures used by both corporate and individual taxpayers that had tax expenditure estimates that were larger or similar in size to the three tax expenditures covered in this report. See GAO, *Corporate Tax Expenditures: Information on Estimated Revenue Losses and Related Federal Spending Programs,* GAO-13-339 (Washington, D.C.: Mar. 18, 2013).

[2] Corporate tax expenditure estimates totaled $147 billion in 2012 while corporate income tax revenue totaled $242 billion. Corporate tax expenditure estimates may be larger relative to corporate income tax revenues due to the continuing effects of a recovering economy as well as bonus depreciation, a temporary provision to stimulate investment, scheduled to expire at the end of 2013. While sufficiently reliable as a gauge of general magnitude, summing tax expenditure estimates does not take into account any interactions between tax expenditures. In addition, tax expenditure estimates do not incorporate any behavioral responses. Thus, they do not represent the revenue amount that would be gained if a specific tax expenditure was repealed.

[3] GAO, *Tax Expenditures: Background and Evaluation Criteria and Questions,* GAO-13-167SP (Washington, D.C.: Nov. 29, 2012). The graduated corporation income tax rate is the terminology used in Treasury's tax expenditure estimates, but we refer to it as the graduated corporate income tax rate schedule or graduated rates for this report.

[4] The SOI corporate sample is not designed to estimate the number of corporations in small subgroups with the exception of groups consisting of only large corporations. In addition, some cells with very small numbers are collapsed or suppressed to protect taxpayer information.

[5] Dividends are only one form of foreign source income. Others can include royalties, license payments, and export income. See CRS, *Moving to a Territorial Income Tax: Options and Challenges* (Washington, D.C.: July 25, 2012).

[6] Lowell D. Yoder, "Subpart F in Turmoil: Low-Taxed Active Income Under Siege" *Taxes*, vol. 77 (March 1999).

[7] PWC identified six countries that have a worldwide tax system with a foreign tax credit. These include the United States, Mexico, the Republic of Korea, Israel, Ireland, and Chile. See PWC, *Evolution of Territorial Tax Systems in the OECD*, prepared for the Technology CEO Council (Apr. 2, 2013).

[8] GAO, *International Taxation: Study Countries That Exempt Foreign-Source Income Face Compliance Risks and Burdens Similar to Those in the United States,* GAO-09-934 (Washington, D.C.: Sept. 15, 2009).

[9] Once reached, the two highest brackets give corporations an average tax rate of 34 and 35 percent, respectively.

[10] The concept of tax expenditures extends beyond the income tax. Tax expenditures also exist for other types of taxes, such as excise and payroll taxes. However, this report considers only tax expenditures for the federal income tax system. Different tax expenditures would apply in the case of a consumption tax.

[11] Both Treasury and JCT use judgment when establishing their normal baseline tax structures. It is sometimes the case that a particular provision is considered an exception to the baseline structure and another, very similar provision is not. For example, graduated rates for C corporations are considered an exception, while S corporation provisions that can also provide lower tax rates for businesses are not. Treasury also discusses an alternative baseline tax structure—the reference tax baseline—which defines as tax expenditures only

those provisions that are special exceptions from a generally defined tax rule that serves programmatic functions similar to spending programs. The general deferral provision and the graduated rates are not considered to be tax expenditures relative to this baseline. In addition, in 2008, JCT did not consider either of the deferral provisions as tax expenditures under a new approach for considering tax expenditures used only in that year. See JCT, *Estimates of Federal Tax Expenditures for Fiscal Years 2008-2027*, JCS-2-08 (Washington, D.C.: Oct. 31, 2008).

[12] Office of Management and Budget (OMB), *Analytical Perspectives, Budget of the United States Government, Fiscal Year 2014* (Washington, D.C.: 2013); and JCT, *Estimates of Federal Tax Expenditures for Fiscal Years 2012-2017*, JCS-1-13 (Washington, D.C.: Feb. 1, 2013).

[13] While, in general, the tax expenditure lists Treasury and JCT publish annually are similar, they differ somewhat in the number of tax expenditures reported, and the estimated revenue losses for particular expenditures. The organizations use different (1) income tax baselines; (2) de minimis amounts, which is the minimum revenue loss threshold for Treasury and JCT to report a tax expenditure; and (3) economic and technical assumptions. For more information on how Treasury and JCT estimate revenue loss, see appendix III of GAO, *Government Performance and Accountability: Tax Expenditures Represent a Substantial Federal Commitment and Need to Be Reexamined,* GAO-05-690 (Washington, D.C.: Sept. 23, 2005).

[14] As the Congressional Research Service (CRS) points out in its tax expenditures compendium, deferral has been part of the U.S. tax system since the creation of the corporate income tax in 1909. See U.S. Congress, Senate Committee on the Budget, *Tax Expenditures: Compendium of Background Material on Individual Provisions*, S. Prt. 111- 58, prepared by CRS (Washington, D.C.: December 2012). Initially, the deferral of tax on the income of controlled foreign corporations may have been meant to delay taxation until a corporation realized income, according to the notion that income should not be taxed before it is available for taxpayer use.

[15] Competitiveness has been identified as the purpose of deferral in parts of the legislative history. Subsequent legislative changes, primarily during the creation of Subpart F, provided a more explicit purpose for deferral. While considering how to restrict deferral through Subpart F in 1962, as well as creating the exception for deferred taxes for certain income earned overseas by financial-services firms, both the House and Senate reports recognized deferral was needed to help maintain active American business operations abroad on an equal competitive footing with other businesses operating overseas. See H.R. Rep. No. 87-1447, 62 (1962); S. Rep. No. 87-1881, at 83 (1962). See also H.R. Conf. Rep. No. 105-220 644-45 (1997). Changes in Subpart F were also introduced to encourage investment in less developed countries. See Treasury, *The Deferral of Income Earned Through U.S. Controlled Foreign Corporations: A Policy Study* (Washington, D.C.: December 2000).

[16] Other factors, such as differences in regulatory and trade frameworks, may provide incentives to invest abroad as well. See Mihir A. Desai, C. Fritz Foley, and James R. Hines Jr., "Domestic Effects of the Foreign Activities of U.S. Multinationals," *American Economic Journal: Economic Policy* (2009), Martin Sullivan, "Economic Analysis: Will Obama's International Proposals Kill U.S. Jobs?", *Tax Notes Today* (June 1, 2009), and Harry Grubert, "Foreign Taxes and The Growing Share of U.S. Multinational Company Income Abroad: Profits, Not Sales, Are Being Globalized," *National Tax Journal*, vol. 65 (June 2012).

[17] See Nicola Satori and Reuven S. Avi-Yonah, "Symposium on International Taxation and Competitiveness: Foreword," *Tax Law Review*, vol. 65 (Spring 2012). This paper summarizes a variety of viewpoints on competitiveness.

[18] A number of tax expenditures benefit U.S. corporations that produce domestically, such as the inventory property sales source rules exception and the deduction for U.S. production activities, although both have tax expenditure estimates smaller than the general deferral provision. See OMB, *Analytical Perspectives, Budget of the United States Government, Fiscal Year 2014* (Washington, D.C.: 2013).

[19] GAO, *U.S. Multinational Corporations: Effective Tax Rates Are Correlated with Where Income Is Reported,* GAO-08-950 (Washington, D.C.: Aug. 12, 2008). Deferral reduces U.S. multinational corporations' effective tax rate. The present value of a tax paid in the future is generally less than that of a tax paid today because the taxpayer can then use the funds (for example, for investment) until the tax is paid. These funds would have been unavailable to the taxpayer had the tax been paid earlier.

[20] See Kevin S. Markle and Douglas Shackelford, "Do Multinationals or Domestic Firms Face Higher Effective Tax Rates?," *National Bureau of Economic Research Working Paper Series* (June 2009).

[21] See Eric Toder, "International Competiveness: Who Competes Against Whom and for What?," *Tax Law Review*, vol. 65 (Spring 2012).

[22] See Michael S. Knoll, "The Connection Between Competitiveness and International Taxation," *Tax Law Review*, vol. 65 (Spring 2012).

[23] The concept of economic efficiency is described in more detail later in this report.

[24] See Jane G. Gravelle, "Does the Concept of Competitiveness Have Meaning in Formulating Corporate Tax Policy?," *Tax Law Review*, vol. 65 (Spring 2012).

[25] See GAO-13-167SP for a more detailed discussion of economic efficiency. Also see appendix II of this report for an example of how these inefficiencies can occur when taxes affect how taxpayers make investment decisions.

[26] CRS, among others, outlined a number of other considerations that may have to be evaluated if a move to a territorial tax system was implemented. CRS, *Moving to a Territorial Income Tax: Options and Challenges* (Washington, D.C.: July 15, 2012).

[27] Organisation for Economic Co-operation and Development, *Tax Effects on Foreign Direct Investment: Recent Evidence and Policy Analysis: Tax Policy Study No. 17* (2007).

[28] Change of incorporation may occur through a corporate inversion or cross-border merger and acquisition. See Johannes Voget, "Relocation of Headquarters and International Taxation," *Journal of Public Economics*, vol. 95 (October 2011).

[29] Jim A. Seida and William F. Wempe, "Effective Tax Rate Changes and Earning Stripping Following Corporate Inversion," *National Tax Journal,* vol. 57 (December 2004).

[30] Eric J. Allen and Susan C. Morse, "Tax-Haven Incorporation For U.S.-Headquartered Firms: No Exodus Yet," *National Tax Journal*, vol. 66 (June 2013); Martin Sullivan, "Economic Analysis: Another Pharmaceutical Inversion to Ireland; More on the Horizon?", *Tax Notes Today* (Aug. 8, 2013); and Bret Wells, "Cant and the Inconvenient Truth About Corporate Inversions," *Tax Notes Today* (July 5, 2012).

[31] The American Jobs Creation Act of 2004 (P.L. 108-357) was targeted at restricting corporate inversion. See CRS, *Firms That Incorporate Abroad for Tax Purposes: Corporate inversions" and "Expatriation*" (Washington, D.C.: Mar. 5, 2010).

[32] Mihir A. Desai and James Hines, "Evaluating International Tax Reform," *National Tax Journal*, vol. 46 (September 2003).

[33] CRS, *Reform of U.S. International Taxation: Alternatives* (Washington, D.C.: Dec. 27, 2012).

[34] Mihir A. Desai, C. Fritz Foley, and James R. Hines, "Repatriation Taxes and Dividend Distortions," *National Tax Journal,* vol. 54 (December 2001); and Harry Grubert and John Mutti, *Taxing International Business Income: Dividend Exemption versus the Current System* (Washington, D.C.: American Enterprise Institute) (2001).

[35] The American Jobs Creation Act of 2004, section 422, allowed companies to pay a onetime 5.25-percent tax rate on repatriated foreign earnings. Companies brought back $312 billion into the United States due to this change. See IRS, *The One-Time Received Dividend Deduction,* SOI Bulletin (Spring 2008).

[36] Harry Grubert and Rosanne Altshuler, *Fixing the System: An Analysis of Alternative Proposals for the Reform of International Tax,* Working Papers Series (Apr. 1, 2013).

[37] See IRS, *The One-Time Received Dividend Deduction,* SOI Bulletin (Spring 2008).

[38] Most experts agree that the scope for income shifting and the resulting compliance and administrative burden have increased by the check-the-box regulations and the look-through provision of the IRC. The check-the-box regulations, issued by Treasury in 1997, permit U.S. taxpayers to treat certain wholly owned foreign entities either as separate corporations or to "disregard" them as unincorporated branches simply by checking a box on a tax form. Taxpayers have used this flexibility to create "hybrid entities," which are business operations treated as corporations by one country's tax authority, and as unincorporated branch operations by another's. See 26 C.F.R. §§ 301.7701-1 to 4. Congress passed the look-through rules in 2006. The rules allow dividends, interest, rents, and royalties received or accrued by one controlled foreign corporation from a related controlled foreign corporation not to be treated as Subpart F income and thus eligible for deferral. See 26 U.S.C. § 954(c)(6).

[39] The complexity of Subpart F has increased with the inclusion of the check-the-box regulations and the look-through rules discussed above.

[40] GAO, *International Taxation: Study Countries That Exempt Foreign-Source Income Face Compliance Risks and Burdens Similar to Those in the United States,* GAO-09-934 (Washington, D.C.: Sept. 15, 2009).

[41] The foreign tax credit also adds complexity when U.S. corporations try to time their repatriations to claim as much of the credit as possible. Corporations can lower the amount of U.S. tax they would otherwise have to pay by repatriating income from low-tax countries when they have excess foreign tax credits. The corporation uses cross-crediting where it applies excess foreign tax credits generated in a high-tax country to the U.S. tax owed on income generated in a low-tax country. Corporations, however, are not allowed to use excess credits associated with passive income to offset taxes on active income, or vice versa.

[42] See GAO-13-339.

[43] GAO, *2013 Annual Report: Actions Needed to Reduce Fragmentation, Overlap, and Duplication and Achieve Other Financial Benefits,* GAO-13-279SP (Washington, D.C.: Apr. 9, 2013).

[44] Over the 5-period from 2012 to 2016, CBO reports that the total estimated revenue effects of moving to a full inclusion worldwide system would be $49.7 billion, while the effect of moving to a territorial system would be $31.7 billion. These estimates were prepared for the CBO report by staff of JCT. For more details on the estimates, see CBO, *Reducing the Deficit: Spending and Revenue Options* (Washington, D.C.: Mar. 10, 2011). If estimates of the revenue effects of moving to a worldwide tax system more current than CBO's 2011 estimates were made, there is some evidence that they could be larger. JCT's tax expenditure estimates increased substantially after this revenue estimate was made,

increasing from $15.6 billion to $36.6 billion in constant 2012 dollars. Although, as pointed out earlier, tax expenditure estimates do not include behavioral responses, the increase in the tax expenditure estimate may indicate a larger revenue impact if the U.S. moved to a full inclusion worldwide system.

[45] JCT notes that its corporate tax model for estimating revenue effects includes possible behavioral changes in: (1) corporate dividends and retained earnings; (2) the corporate capital structure; (3) corporate equity valuations; (4) repatriations of deferred foreign income; and (5) business entity choice. See JCT, *Summary of Economic Models and Estimating Practices of the Staff of the Joint Committee on Taxation*. (Washington, D.C.: Sept. 19, 2011). JCT's revenue estimates prepared for specific proposals differ from its and Treasury's tax expenditure estimates that do not incorporate such behavioral responses. For an explanation of how JCT and Treasury complete their tax expenditure estimates, see JCT, *Estimates of Federal Tax Expenditures for Fiscal Years 2012-2017*, JCS-1-13 (Washington, D.C.: Feb. 1, 2013), and OMB, *Analytical Perspectives, Budget of the United States Government*, Fiscal Year 2014 (Washington, D.C.: 2013).

[46] Overhead costs, such as interest expenses, of a U.S. parent corporation would be allocated between the company's U.S. and foreign activities, as is the case under current law for purposes of computing the foreign tax credit. In a departure from current law, however, overhead expenses allocated to foreign income would no longer be deductible from U.S. income. As noted by CBO, the net increase in revenues when the dividend exemption system is adopted occurs because revenues lost by exempting active dividends from U.S. taxation would be more than offset by increases in taxes because overhead expenses allocated to exempt foreign income could no longer be deducted from U.S. income. If the tax treatment of overhead expenses was not altered, moving to a dividend exemption system may entail a reduction in the tax revenue the federal government collects from corporations.

[47] GAO, *International Taxation: Study Countries That Exempt Foreign-Source Income Face Compliance Risks and Burdens Similar to Those in the United States,* GAO-09-934 (Washington, D.C.: Sept. 15, 2009).

[48] Treasury estimated that revenue losses from the deferral of income for controlled foreign corporations rose from about $7.7 billion in 1999 to $42 billion in 2012. The difference in the estimation methods is illustrated by the 2012 estimated revenue loss of $42 billion, and JCT's estimate of a $4.7 billion revenue gain for a specific proposal to adopt full inclusion. Estimates for deferred taxes for financial firms on certain income earned overseas during a similar period show revenue losses increasing at a slower pace, from $1.3 billion to $2.5 billion during the same period. As we pointed out in our prior work on corporate tax expenditures, the general deferral provision was the second largest in terms of tax expenditure estimates, behind only accelerated depreciation of machinery and equipment. See GAO-13-339.

[49] The Tax Increase Prevention and Reconciliation Act ("TIPRA") of 2005 (H.R. 4297), enacted on May 17, 2006 (Pub. L. No. 109-222).

[50] Lee Sheppard and Martin Sullivan, "News Analysis: Multinationals Accumulate to Repatriate," *Tax Notes Today* (January 15, 2009).

[51] GAO, *Tax Policy: Tax Expenditures Deserve More Scrutiny*, GAO/GGD/AIMD-94-122 (Washington, D.C.: June 3, 1994), and *Government Performance and Accountability: Tax Expenditures Represent a Substantial Federal Commitment and Need to Be Reexamined,* GAO-05-690 (Washington, D.C.: Sept. 23, 2005).

[52] GAO, *Managing For Results: Executive Branch Should More Fully Implement the GPRA Modernization Act to Address Pressing Governance Challenges,* GAO-13-518 (Washington, D.C.: June 26, 2013).

[53] See also OMB Circular No. A-11 (July 2013).

[54] The benefit that the graduated corporate income tax rates provide is taken back in the form of higher rates when the corporation's income exceeds the graduated rate income range.

[55] U.S. Congress, Senate Committee on the Budget, *Tax Expenditures: Compendium of Background Material on Individual Provisions*, S. Prt. 112-45, prepared by CRS (Washington, D.C.: December 2012).

[56] See Simeon Djankov, Tim Ganser, Caralee McLiesh, Rita Ramalho, and Andrei Shleifer, "The Effect of Corporate Taxes on Investment and Entrepreneurship," *American Economic Journal: Macroeconomics,* vol. 2 (July 2010); and Julie Berry Cullen and Roger H. Gordon, "Taxes and entrepreneurial risk-taking: Theory and evidence for the U.S," *Journal of Public Economics*, vol. 91 (2007).

[57] Asli Demirguc-Kunt, Inessa Love, and Vojislav Maksimovic, "Business Environment and the Incorporation Decision," *Journal of Banking and Finance*, vol. 30 (2006).

[58] Matthew J. Knittel and Susan C. Nelson, "How Would Small Business Owners Fare Under a Business Entity Tax," *National Tax Journal*, vol. 64 (December 2011).

[59] These data represent a snapshot of IRS data, and may not be representative of trends before and after the economic recession that occurred from December 2007 to June 2009.

[60] We made a number of recommendations to OMB, which included that it provide guidance to agencies to identify tax expenditures that contribute to each appropriate agency goal. OMB agreed with the recommendations we made. See GAO-13-518.

[61] Treasury, *Taxes and Corporate Choice of Organizational Form* (Washington, D.C.: 1997).

[62] The effect of graduated rates on organizational form is difficult to determine because, in part, businesses have a variety of organizational forms available that affect their tax liabilities. For example, besides C corporations, they can organize as "pass-through" entities such as partnerships and S corporations that pay the individual tax rate and avoid the double tax on corporate dividends.

[63] For more details on these studies of the impact of small businesses, see CRS' recently issued comprehensive study. CRS, *Small Business Tax Benefits: Current Law and Main Arguments For and Against Them* (Washington, D.C.: Mar. 11, 2013).

[64] The question of who receives the benefit of the tax expenditure—referred to as the incidence of the benefit —is explored in more detail in GAO-13-167SP.

[65] Tax net income represents a firm's taxable income before subtracting any net operating loss carryforward or special deductions and is most closely comparable to domestic pretax book income. The most dramatic changes occurred in corporations currently in the zero-, 25- , 34- , and 38-percent tax brackets, all of which face a different marginal tax rate from a 5-percent increase in tax net income. See IRS, *The Distribution of Corporate Income: Tabulations from the Schedule M-3, 2004-2008*, SOI Bulletin (Washington, D.C.: Spring 2012).

[66] See Donald DeLuca, John Guyton, Wu-Lang Lee, John O'Hare, and Scott Stilmar, *Aggregate Estimates of Small Business Taxpayer Compliance Burden,* IRS Research Bulletin (2007).

[67] See GAO-13-339.

[68] GAO, *Entrepreneurial Assistance: Opportunities Exist to Improve Programs Collaboration, Data Track, and Performance Management,* GAO-12-819 (Washington, D.C.: Aug. 23, 2012).

[69] From 2012 to 2016, the revenue effects of this option would be $12.1 billion. The staff of the JCT prepared most of the revenue estimates in CBO's report. See CBO, *Reducing the Deficit: Spending and Revenue Options* (Washington, D.C.: Mar. 10, 2011).

[70] GAO, *Managing For Results: Executive Branch Should More Fully Implement the GPRA Modernization Act to Address Pressing Governance Challenges,* GAO-13-518 (Washington, D.C.: June 26, 2013).

[71] See also OMB Circular No. A-11 (July 2013).

End Notes for Appendix I

[1] GAO, *Tax Expenditures: Background and Evaluation Criteria and Questions,* GAO-13- 167SP (Washington, D.C.: Nov. 29, 2012)

[2] U.S. Congress, Senate Committee on the Budget, *Tax Expenditures: Compendium of Background Material on Individual Provisions*, S. Prt. 111-58, prepared by CRS (Washington, D.C.: December 2010) and U.S. Congress, Senate Committee on Finance, *Economic Efficiency and Structural Analyses of Alternative U.S. Tax Policies For Foreign Direct Investment*. Prepared by JCT (Washington, D.C.: June 2008).

[3] We chose 1998 as the first year as that was the first year Treasury estimated revenue losses for deferred taxes for financial firms on certain income earned overseas since the exception was eliminated in 1986. See 26 U.S.C. § 954(h), which was added by the Taxpayer Relief Act of 1997, Pub. L. No 105-34 § 1175 (Aug. 5, 1997).

[4] Treasury estimates the portion of revenue losses associated with corporate or individual taxpayers for each tax expenditure in its list. However, all three tax expenditures in the scope of our report only have tax expenditure estimates for corporate taxpayers.

[5] See CBO, *Reducing the Deficit: Spending and Revenue Options* (Washington, D.C.: Mar. 10, 2011).

[6] See JCT, *Summary of Economic Models and Estimating Practices of the Staff of the Joint Committee on Taxation* (Washington, D.C.: Sept. 19, 2011).

[7] Mihir A. Desai and James R. Hines Jr., "Old Rules and New Realities: Corporate Tax Policy in a Global Setting," *National Tax Journal*, vol. 57 (December 2004).

End Notes for Appendix II

[1] Harry Grubert and Rosanne Altshuler, *Fixing the System: An Analysis of Alternative Proposals for the Reform of International Tax*, Working Papers Series (Apr. 1, 2013) and CRS, *Reform of U.S. International Taxation: Alternatives* (Washington, D.C.: Dec. 27, 2012).

[2] If the U.S. tax rate is lower than the foreign tax rate, the U.S. system, which limits the foreign tax credit to the U.S. tax liability on the foreign income, discourages investment abroad. See Organisation for Economic Co-operation and Development, *Tax Effects on Foreign Direct Investment: Recent Evidence and Policy Analysis. Tax Policy Study No. 17* (2007).

[3] Harry Grubert. "Foreign Taxes and the Growing Share of U.S. Multinational Company Income Abroad: Profits, Not Sales, Are Being Globalized," *National Tax Journal*, vol. 65 (June 2012). The author argues that income shifting may be growing due to tax-planning opportunities that were increased by check-the-box-rules in 1997.

[4] The incentive to shift income disappears, except for companies that have excess credits.

[5] GAO, *International Taxation: Study Countries That Exempt Foreign-Source Income Face Compliance Risks and Burdens Similar to Those in the United States,* GAO-09-934 (Washington, D.C.: Sept. 15, 2009).

In: Corporate Taxes
Editor: Brianne Nathanson

ISBN: 978-1-63321-922-9

Chapter 3

INTERNATIONAL TAXATION: STUDY COUNTRIES THAT EXEMPT FOREIGN-SOURCE INCOME FACE COMPLIANCE RISKS AND BURDENS SIMILAR TO THOSE IN THE UNITED STATES*

United States Government Accountability Office

WHY GAO DID THIS STUDY

A debate is underway about how the United States should tax foreign-source, corporate income. Currently, the United States allows domestic corporations to defer tax on the earnings of their foreign subsidiaries and also gives credits for foreign taxes paid, while most other developed countries exempt the active earnings of their multinational corporations' foreign subsidiaries from domestic tax. The debate has focused on economic issues with little attention to tax administration. GAO was asked to describe for a group of study countries with exemption systems: (1) the rules for exempting foreign-source income, and (2) the compliance risk and taxpayer compliance burden, such as recordkeeping, of the rules. The study countries, selected to provide a range of exemption systems, are Australia, Canada, France,

* This is an edited, reformatted and augmented version of the United States Government Accountability Office publication, GAO-09-934, dated September 2009.

Germany, and the Netherlands. For these countries GAO reviewed documents; interviewed government officials, academic experts, and business representatives; and compared tax policies, compliance activities and taxpayer reporting requirements.

GAO Recommends

Because changing the United States system of taxing foreign-source income is a policy decision, GAO is not making recommendations related to tax reform. GAO does recommend that the Secretary of Treasury annually report, using already available data, the revenue generated by taxing foreign-source corporate income. The Secretary agreed with our recommendation.

What GAO Found

The study countries exempt some corporate income, such as dividends received from foreign subsidiaries, from domestic tax. However, the study countries tax other types of foreign-source income such as royalties.

Multinational corporations present a compliance risk because they can use subsidiaries to convert taxable income into tax-exempt or lower taxed income, eroding the domestic tax base. Although quantitative estimates of noncompliance do not exist, tax experts interviewed by GAO identified sources of compliance risk and taxpayer burden in each of the study countries. These issues, particularly the ones below, have also been identified as sources of compliance risk and burden in the United States.

Transfer prices—the prices for transactions between related parties—can be manipulated to shift profits. Tax experts in the study countries said the growing importance of intangible property such as trademarks and patents is making international transactions more susceptible to transfer pricing abuse. In response, the study countries have all increased their scrutiny of transfer prices, including increased demands for documentation and more audits, resulting in increased compliance burden for taxpayers. Cooperative efforts between taxpayers and tax agencies to reduce audits, such as Advanced Pricing Agreements, received mixed reviews in the study countries.

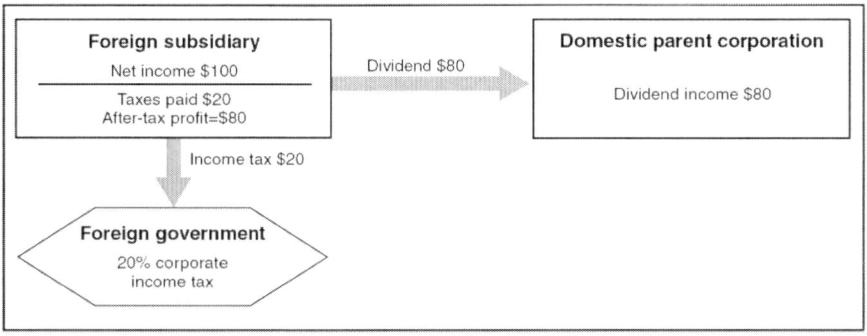

Simple Example of Dividend Exemption.

Anti-avoidance rules prevent taxpayers from moving passive income (interest and royalties are often passive income) to a foreign subsidiary in order to avoid domestic tax. Generally, the rules make such passive income, even if moved, taxable. Tax agencies and taxpayers reported difficulties in obtaining information from other countries to make complex determinations about whether the anti-avoidance rules apply or not.

The United States does not report taxes paid on foreign-source income. Treasury officials said it would be feasible to do so. Such reporting would make more explicit the role international tax rules play in raising revenues and protecting the domestic tax base. All experts we spoke with on this topic agreed.

***

September 15, 2009

The Honorable Max Baucus
Chairman
The Honorable Charles E. Grassley
Ranking Member
Committee on Finance
United States Senate

One hallmark of the global economy is greater mobility of income and economic transactions. As technology advances and globalization continues to eliminate barriers to conducting business across countries, companies routinely earn income in several countries. For example, U.S. corporations reported $205 billion in foreign-source income for tax year 2003, the latest year currently available.[1] This is about half of the $425 billion of total worldwide income (foreign plus domestic) earned by U.S. corporations in that year.[2] Often income is not earned directly by a domestic corporation, but rather through wholly or partially owned subsidiaries incorporated in other countries.

Foreign-source income, especially when earned by multinational corporations (MNC), presents challenges for income tax design and administration. These challenges include ensuring tax law compliance, minimizing tax induced distortions of businesses decisions about where to locate investment, avoiding the double taxation of income earned in one country by companies located in another country, and minimizing unnecessary taxpayer compliance burden, such as recordkeeping.

There are two general approaches to taxing foreign-source corporate income. Under both approaches, a corporation pays any tax due in the foreign country where the income is earned. The approaches differ in how the corporation is taxed domestically, that is, in the corporation's home country. One approach—called worldwide taxation—taxes all income earned by a corporation regardless of where the income is derived. Under this approach, double taxation is addressed through foreign tax credits (FTC). The FTC is a credit, usually subject to limits, against domestic tax for foreign taxes paid. A corporation would pay domestic tax on foreign- source income only to the extent that the domestic tax on that income exceeds the foreign tax credit.

The other approach—called territorial taxation—only taxes the corporation's income derived within the taxing country's borders, irrespective of the residence of the taxpayer. Thus, unlike worldwide taxation, foreign-source income earned by a domestic corporation is exempt from residence-country tax. The exemption generally eliminates the possibility of double taxation.[3]

In practice, large developed countries do not use a pure worldwide or pure territorial approach when taxing foreign-source corporate income. Instead, they use hybrid approaches. Most developed countries, especially after recent policy changes in Japan and the United Kingdom, now lean toward a territorial approach but are not purely territorial—in part, because they place significant limitations on what types of income are eligible for exempt treatment.[4] The United States and a few other countries, on the other hand, lean toward a more worldwide approach but are not purely worldwide—in part, because taxation can be deferred on certain qualifying income until it is actually paid to the domestic corporation by subsidiaries as dividends. Basic features of the U.S.

tax system result in the ability of some MNCs to defer domestic taxation until it is actually paid to a domestic part of the MNC.[5]

In the United States, proposals have been developed to reform the taxation of foreign-source income.[6] The proposals differ, with some designed to move the United States toward more territoriality and others intended to maintain a more worldwide approach. An extensive body of literature debates the economic merits of these proposals, including the effects of taxes on competitiveness and the location decisions of firms. While some research shows that taxes change location incentives, the existing research does not reach definitive conclusions about important economic effects such as the impact of foreign investment by U.S. corporations on U.S. employment.

Compared to the extensive examination of economic effects, little has been done to study whether there are important differences between worldwide and territorial systems in terms of tax administration and, more specifically, in terms of compliance by taxpayers and taxpayers' compliance burden (recordkeeping, reporting, and other costs). In the context of foreign-source income, at least two broad compliance issues exist. One is ensuring that domestic corporations pay the tax due on foreign-source income. The other is ensuring corporations do not erode the domestic tax base by illegally shifting domestic income abroad.

Because of the ongoing debate about the taxation of foreign-source income and because of the limited information available on administering a worldwide system versus a territorial system, you asked us to report on other countries' experience administering territorial systems. Based on your request, our objectives are to (1) describe, for select case study countries that take a territorial approach, what types of foreign-source income the countries exempt and the rules governing those exemptions; and (2) describe, to the extent information is available, the compliance risks and taxpayer compliance burdens that the taxation of foreign-source corporate income presents for each of these countries.

To address our objectives, we selected five countries—Australia, Canada, France, Germany, and the Netherlands—to study based on several criteria, including range of rules governing the taxation of foreign-source income, unique tax system features, and Organization of Economic Cooperation and Development (OECD) membership. To provide assurance that all of the information used in this report is sufficiently reliable, we used data from commonly used and cited sources of statistical data, such as the OECD, and other publicly available reports from international government agencies. Additionally, we performed an in-depth literature review on all of the study countries, including government documents, private sector studies, and academic publications. We collected and analyzed data on the countries and their systems for taxing foreign-source corporate income, including tax policies, administrative mechanisms, compliance activities, and taxpayer reporting and documentation requirements. We interviewed knowledgeable government officials from the study countries, including officials from the tax agencies. We also interviewed U.S. tax agency officials, international tax experts, including academic and private-sector experts, and members of a number of professional services organizations that represent and serve MNCs that have large numbers of foreign subsidiaries under their control. We provided the tax agencies of our study countries a copy of our report to verify data and specific factual and legal statements about the tax treatment of foreign-source income in those countries. We did not conduct a formal legal review of the tax laws and rules in other countries, but relied on the information supplied by tax agency officials in those countries. We made technical corrections to our report based on these reviews. A more detailed discussion of our methodology is in appendix I.

We conducted our work from June 2008 to September 2009 in accordance with all sections of GAO's Quality Assurance Framework that are relevant to our objectives. The framework requires that we plan and perform the engagement to obtain sufficient and appropriate evidence to meet our stated objectives and to discuss any limitations in our work. We believe that the information and data obtained, and the analysis conducted, provide a reasonable basis for any findings and conclusions in this product.

BACKGROUND

Multinational Corporations and Foreign-Source Income

Corporate income tax is levied on business entities that organize and operate as corporations, as defined by each individual country's tax rules and laws. Generally, corporations are individual business entities that issue shares and can make distributions to shareholders, such as dividend payments.

Corporations can be shareholders in other corporations, both domestic and foreign. The amount of control the corporate shareholder has over the other corporation can vary depending on the percentage of shares owned and other factors. At the low range of corporate ownership, portfolio shareholding allows a corporate shareholder to invest in a business but does not involve maintaining a controlling stake in the firm. At greater levels of ownership, corporations can own a sufficient percentage of shares to gain partial or total control of major business decisions, such as the level and timing of dividend distributions and investment and pricing strategies. For this report, we will call the controlling firm a parent corporation and the controlled firm a subsidiary.[7] Parent-subsidiary relationships can be complicated, involving a corporation owning multiple subsidiaries, subsidiaries being controlled by multiple parents, or tiered arrangements with subsidiaries owning subsidiaries of their own. When these relationships involve entities in more than one country, these corporations are referred to as multinational corporations (MNC).

MNCs are groups of separate legal entities, which can include corporations, partnerships, trusts, and other legal entities, that operate and generate income in multiple countries, and different parts of an MNC may have different domestic jurisdictions. MNCs may also have branches—domestic, foreign, or both—as part of a corporation's internal organizational structure.[8] In general, each corporate entity that is part of the MNC is taxed as an individual taxable entity by the relevant governments, unless the corporation is allowed to and chooses to file a consolidated return.

Different Types of Foreign- Source Income

Corporations can earn a variety of different types of income from foreign sources. This income can be generated from transactions with either unrelated parties, such as retail customers located abroad, or related parties, such as foreign subsidiaries or other parts of the same MNC. Corporations can earn foreign-source income from active and passive activities with foreign parties. While countries vary somewhat in their definitions of active and passive income, generally speaking, active income is considered to be the income generated through the primary business activities of the corporation. Passive income, in contrast, is income that is not earned through primary business activities. Interest earned, rental income, and royalty payments from foreign sources are generally considered passive income. However, for some companies, such as financial services companies, these types of income may constitute the primary business and be considered active income under the tax laws of some countries. Additionally, corporations can purchase shares of foreign companies and receive dividend distributions based on the earnings of those companies. Table 1 below lists some general examples of different types of income that can be generated from foreign-sources.

Table 1. Select Examples of Types of Income That Can Be Generated from Foreign Sources[a]

Type of income	General definition	Example of foreign-source income in a parent-subsidiary relationship
Capital gains	The gain realized from the appreciated value between the purchase and sales price of an asset, such as shares in a corporation. Investments that have not yet been sold, but would yield a profit if they were sold have unrealized capital gains.	A domestic parent sells shares it held in a foreign subsidiary for $50. The domestic parent had bought the shares for $20. The realized capital gain is the $30 difference.
Dividends	A payment distributed by a company to its shareholders. Dividends are usually given out in the form of cash, but can also be given out as stock or other property.	A domestic parent company owns 10,000 shares of a foreign subsidiary. The foreign subsidiary makes a dividend payment of $1 per share to all shareholders, including $10,000 to the parent.
Interest	Payments received as compensation for lending money.	A domestic parent makes a 10-year, 5 percent loan for $1 million to a foreign subsidiary. The subsidiary makes semi-annual interest payments of $25,000 to the domestic parent.
Rent	Compensation for the use or occupation of property.	A domestic parent owns a factory in a foreign country. A foreign subsidiary makes monthly payments to the domestic parent for occupation and use of the factory.
Royalty	Income generated from licensing the use of property, such as intellectual property.	A foreign subsidiary pays a domestic parent firm for the right to use trademark logos on goods produced and sold.

Source: GAO

[a] The definitions in this chart reflect how we use these terms for the purposes of this report. Other definitions exist for these terms but are outside the scope of this report.

Most Countries Take a Hybrid Approach to Taxing Foreign-Source Income

In practice, countries combine elements of worldwide and territorial approaches to taxing foreign-source income. One approach, generally referred to as deferral, deviates from the worldwide model and taxes the domestic corporation on all of its income, including income and dividends received from foreign subsidiaries, but defers taxation until the income is repatriated. Another approach, generally referred to as dividend exemption, is closer to the territorial model and permits the tax-exempt repatriation of the dividends distributed by foreign subsidiaries, but may limit the extent to which some income is exempt. In either system, foreign- source income is taxed first in the source country; under a deferral system, a residual tax is then imposed only when the income is repatriated. Figure 1 shows a continuum of tax treatments for foreign-source corporate income with hybrid systems ranging between the pure worldwide and territorial models.

Worldwide System with Deferral

The current tax system in the United States is an example of a worldwide system with deferral, which taxes domestic corporations on their worldwide income, regardless of where the income is earned and gives credits for foreign income taxes paid. Income unrelated to a U.S. trade or business earned by foreign corporations is not taxed domestically until it is distributed to a domestic shareholder, such as a domestic parent corporation, which allows deferral of taxation on income of foreign subsidiaries. Special rules may exist that tax certain shareholders, such as a parent corporation, currently on the income of certain subsidiaries in order to protect the domestic tax base. To reduce the double taxation of income, corporate taxpayers can offset, in whole or in part, the domestic tax owed on the foreign-source income through a FTC. In certain circumstances, a parent corporation may claim FTCs for foreign taxes paid by a subsidiary. Figure 2 shows how a dividend payment is generally taxed under a worldwide tax approach that permits deferral.

Exemption Systems

Many OECD countries exempt some types of foreign-source corporate income from domestic tax. Exemptions are commonly granted in these countries for dividends paid by a foreign subsidiary. As shown in figure 3, which is a simplified example of an exemption system, the domestic corporation does not incur a tax liability by receiving the dividend income from its foreign subsidiary. However, similar to the worldwide systems with deferral that were described earlier, exemption systems may disallow the tax advantages of foreign-source income under certain circumstances to protect the domestic tax base.

Study Countries Vary in the Types of Foreign-Source Income Exempted from Domestic Tax and in the Rules Governing Those Exemptions

Our study countries—Australia, Canada, France, Germany, and the Netherlands—have hybrid tax systems that exempt some types of foreign-source income and tax others. All of the study countries tax domestic corporations on income earned through rental payments and royalties. Such payments may be made by unrelated parties or by subsidiaries and are generally expenses of the payee in the foreign country but are received as income by the domestic corporation. Subject to an extensive list of exceptions, the study countries generally exempt, but to varying extents, income of domestic corporations received as foreign-source dividends from foreign subsidiaries, sales by foreign branches, and the gains from the sale of shares in foreign subsidiaries. For example, all of the study countries permit domestic corporations to receive dividends that meet certain qualifications as tax-exempt income, but differ in the rules they use in determining which dividends are qualified. In addition, Canada does not allow domestic corporations to earn tax-exempt, foreign-source income through foreign branches and taxes up to half of the capital gains on the sale of foreign subsidiary shares while the other study countries generally exempt income from these sources.[9]

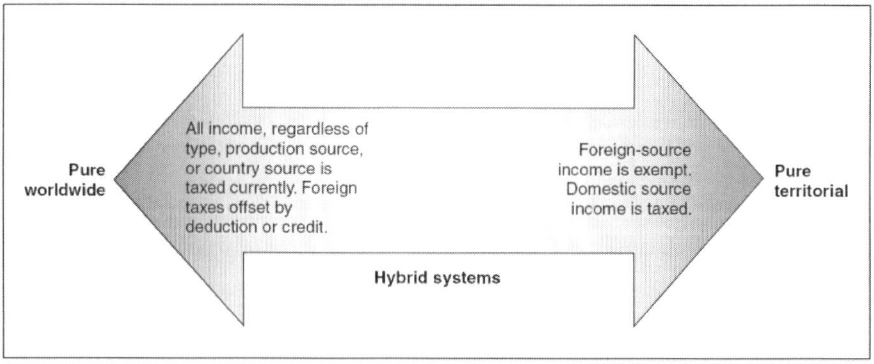

Source: GAO.

Figure 1. Continuum of Tax Systems of Foreign-Source Corporate Income.

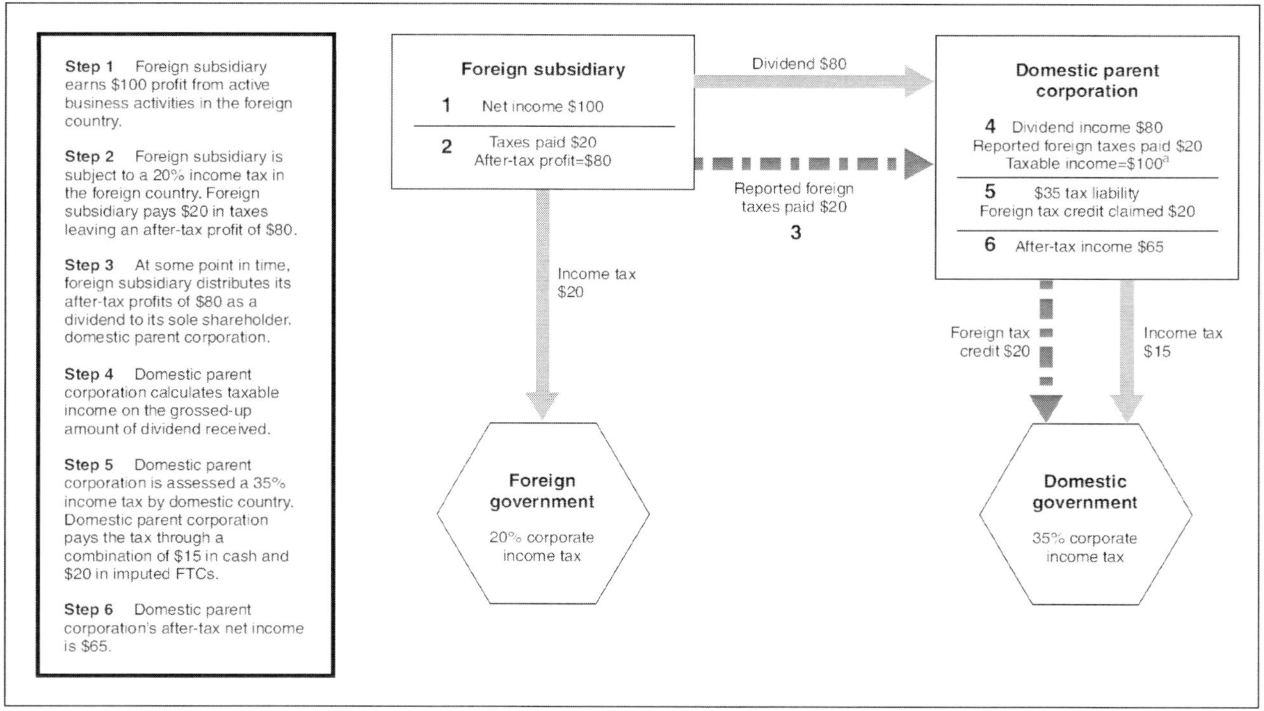

Source: GAO.

[a] Domestic tax liability is based on the grossed-up value of the dividend plus the amount of foreign income tax paid on the associated earnings.

Figure 2. Simple Example of Deferral.

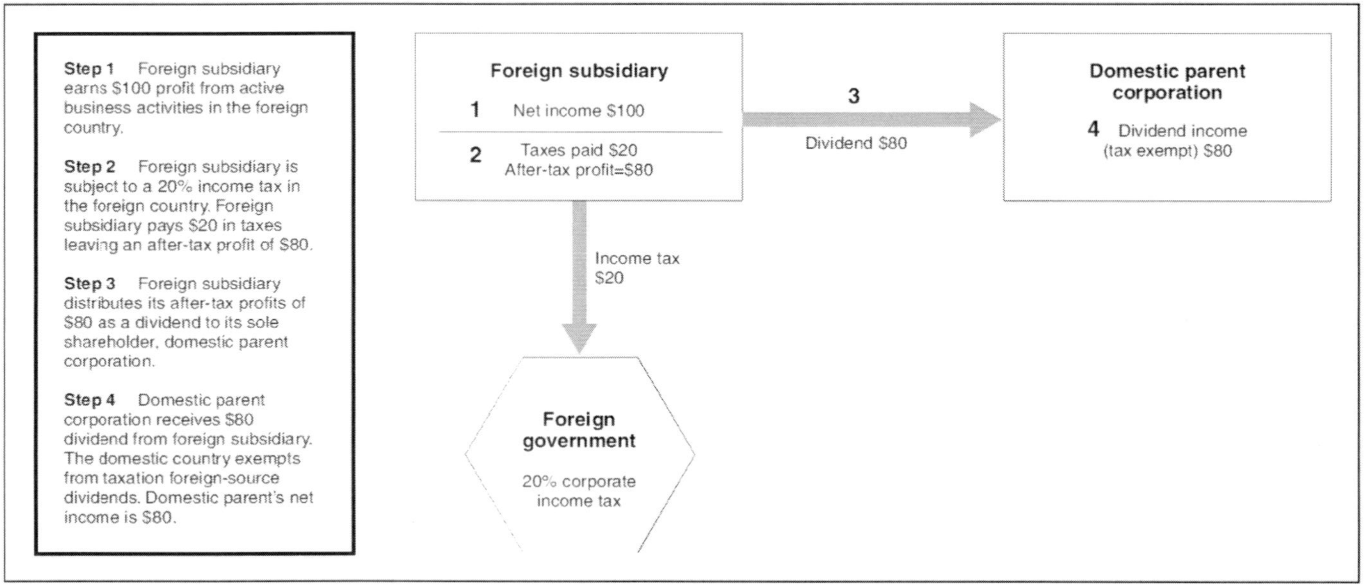

Source: GAO.

Figure 3. Simple Example of Dividend Exemption.

Table 2. General Domestic Tax Treatment of Different Types of Foreign-Source Income

		Australia	Canada	France	Germany	Netherlands
Rent, royalty, and interest income paid by	**Foreign subsidiaries**	Taxable	Taxable	Taxable	Taxable	Taxable
	Unrelated third parties	Taxable	Taxable	Taxable	Taxable	Taxable
Nonqualifying foreign-source dividends		Taxable	Taxable	Taxable	Taxable	Taxable
Qualified foreign-source dividends		Exempt	Exempt	Effectively 95% exempt[a]	Effectively 95% exempt[a]	Exempt
Active foreign branch income		Exempt	Taxable with FTC	Exempt	Taxable with FTC under domestic law but generally exempt through tax treaty	Generally exempt
Capital gains from the sale of foreign subsidiary shares		Generally exempt	50%to 100%Exempt	Effectively 95%exempt[a]	Effectively 95%exempt[a]	Exempt
Attributable foreign earnings subject to anti-avoidance rules		Taxable with FTC	Taxable with FTC	Taxable with FTC	Taxable with FTC	Taxable

Source: GAO analysis of country information.

Note: This table shows general treatments. It does not present all of the details, exceptions, or rules that govern the tax treatment of foreign-source income for our study countries.

[a] For France and Germany, the exempt amount of qualified foreign-source gross dividends and capital gains is effectively 95 percent due to rules that tax 5 percent of the income as nondeductible expenses. This is discussed in more detail later in this report.

In addition to the rules above covering income payments received by domestic corporations, all study countries also have rules that tax domestic corporations on some income at the time it is earned by foreign subsidiaries, regardless of when or if the foreign subsidiary distributes a dividend. These rules, generally referred to as anti-avoidance rules, attribute certain earnings of related foreign entities to domestic corporations in order to limit the tax benefits of holding certain types of income offshore.

Table 2 presents a brief overview of the tax treatment for different types of foreign-source income in our study countries. All rows except the last show the tax treatment of income payments received by a domestic corporation. The last row shows the tax treatment of income at the time it is earned by a foreign subsidiary that is subject to certain anti-avoidance rules regardless of whether the income was distributed as a dividend.

While data was not available for most of our study countries, in Canada, at least 76 percent of foreign-source dividends received by Canadian taxpayers from foreign affiliates from 2000 to 2005 were qualified foreign- source dividends and, therefore, were tax exempt.[10]

Study Countries Use Different Criteria to Qualify Foreign-Source Dividends for Domestic Tax Exemption

Our study countries all have certain criteria that, when met, allow domestic corporations to receive tax-exempt income in the form of dividend payments, called qualified foreign-source dividends in table 2. In each of the countries, all of the criteria must be met for the domestic corporation to receive the foreign-source dividend tax-exempt. If any of the conditions are not met, then the dividend does not qualify for the tax exemption and is, therefore, taxable. Our study countries applied up to three criteria when determining which income is tax-exempt: domestic ownership type and level of foreign subsidiaries; the type of income (active versus passive) distributed as a dividend; and the presence of a tax treaty or similar agreement between the domestic and foreign government where the subsidiary is located and income is earned.

All of our study countries except Germany require the domestic corporation to have a minimum ownership stake in a foreign subsidiary in order to qualify for the benefits of exemption. In general, these minimum ownership level stakes mean that income from portfolio or portfolio-like investment is not exempt. Each country takes a different approach in determining the type of shares that qualify dividend income for exemption with distinctions made on the type of shares and the length of time the shares are held. For example, while Canada requires domestic corporations to own 10 percent or more of any class of shares in the foreign subsidiary, France requires its corporations to own at least 5 percent of a foreign subsidiary's shares.[11] The requirements for each country are summarized in table 3.

In addition to the criteria above, Canada also makes a distinction between dividends distributed from active and passive income, while the other study countries do not, as shown in table 4.

Of all our study countries, currently only Canada requires that the foreign subsidiary be located and earn active income in a designated treaty country in order to qualify for the dividend tax exemption that was shown in table 2. For Canada, a designated treaty country is a country with which Canada either has a tax treaty or a tax information exchange agreement (TIEA). As was noted earlier, at least 76 percent of dividends received by Canadian taxpayers from foreign affiliates between 2000 and 2005 were tax exempt.

Table 3. Dividend Qualification Criteria—Required Domestic Ownership Type and Level of Foreign Subsidiary to Qualify for Tax Exemption of Foreign-Source Dividend Income

	Australia	Canada	France	Germany	Netherlands
Domestic ownership of foreign company	Direct shareholding of at least 10%	Direct ownership of 1% and direct or indirect ownership of at least 10%	At least 5% ownership	None	In principle a share-holding of at least 5%
Foreign company share type	Shares must have a voting interest	Any type	Ownership or participating shares	Any type	Any type
Ownership duration	None	None	2 years	None	None

Source: GAO analysis of country information.

Note: This table shows general treatments. It does not present all of the details, exceptions, or rules that govern the tax treatment of foreign-source income for our study countries.

Table 4. Dividend Qualification Criteria—Domestic Tax Treatment of Foreign-source Dividend Income Distributed from Active and Passive Income

	Australia	Canada	France	Germany	Netherlands
Dividends distributed from active income	Exempt	Exempt	Effectively 95% exempt[a]	Effectively 95% exempt[a]	Exempt
Dividends distributed from passive income	Exempt	Taxable with FTC eligibility[b]	Effectively 95% exempt[a]	Effectively 95% exempt[a]	Exempt

Source: GAO analysis of country information.

Note: This table shows general treatments. It does not present all of the details, exceptions, or rules that govern the tax treatment of foreign-source income for our study countries.

[a] In France and Germany, the gross dividend amount exempt from domestic tax is effectively 95 percent due to rules that tax 5 percent of the gross dividend amount as nondeductible expenses. This is discussed in more detail later in this report.

[b] Income that was previously taxed under anti-avoidance rules may be tax exempt upon repatriation.

Study Countries Limit Tax Advantages of Earning Foreign-Source Income under Certain Conditions

As was shown in the last row of table 2, all study countries have anti-avoidance rules that limit the tax advantages of earning certain types of income abroad. In general, these rules are intended to protect the domestic tax base by preventing taxpayers from avoiding domestic tax on passive or other specific types of income by moving to or holding these types of income in a foreign country. When triggered, these rules require a domestic shareholder to be taxed currently on its pro rata share of certain types of income earned by certain foreign subsidiaries, regardless of when or if that income is distributed to the shareholder.[12] Anti-avoidance rules exist in both worldwide and territorial tax systems, and are in effect in each of our study countries and the United States (commonly known as Subpart F in the United States).

A prominent anti-avoidance rule used by all study countries except the Netherlands applies to controlled foreign corporations (CFC).[13] Each country's

CFC rules vary, but they generally tax domestic shareholders, including shareholding corporations, currently on certain types of income earned by foreign corporations that qualify as controlled by domestic shareholders. This is illustrated in figure 4. This means that the domestic corporation may be taxed on income that it has not received from the foreign corporation (called a deemed dividend in figure 4). This income is taxable when earned by the subsidiary, although CFC rules generally permit the domestic taxpayer to offset some or all of their domestic tax liability through credits on the foreign taxes paid on the income.

Generally, study countries establish criteria in three areas that, when met, define a domestic shareholder's tax liability for certain types of income earned by a foreign corporation under the CFC rules. First, countries define when a foreign corporation is controlled by domestic shareholders. For example, Australia defines a controlled foreign corporation as any foreign corporation that meets either of the following definitions: (1) where five or fewer Australian residents effectively control the foreign corporation or own more than 50 percent of the foreign corporation; or (2) where one Australian entity has an individual ownership of 40 percent or more of the foreign corporation not controlled by another corporation. Second, countries generally set a minimum level of ownership in the foreign corporation that domestic shareholders must meet before being taxed on the foreign corporation's earnings. For example, under Canada's CFC rules, a Canadian shareholder must own at least 10 percent of the foreign corporation to be taxed on certain types of income earned by the foreign corporation. Third, the controlled foreign corporation generally must earn certain types of income that are specified in each country's CFC rules. For example, Germany requires that a CFC earn passive income that is taxed at an effective rate of 25 percent or less by the foreign country before a domestic corporation is required to pay tax on the CFC's earnings.

Once the criteria above are met, domestic shareholders are taxed currently on certain types of attributed income earned by the CFC. Some countries, like Canada, generally limit the taxable foreign earnings to the domestic corporation's pro rata share of passive income.[14] Other countries, like France, tax domestic corporations on their pro rata share of all earnings by the foreign corporation. Table 5 presents a simplified overview of the CFC rules used by our study countries. Additional details on other types of anti-avoidance rules can be found in appendix IV.

Table 5. General Overview of CFC and Other Anti-avoidance Rules

	Australia	Canada	France	Germany	Netherlands
Criteria a foreign entity must meet to be considered a CFC	Either: (1) five or fewer Australian residents control or own more than 50%of the foreign entity; or (2) When one Australian resident owns 40%or more of the foreign entity	Five or fewer Canadian residents, including parties that do not deal at arm's length with them, own greater than 50%of the foreign entity	(1) The foreign entity is located in a country with an effective tax rate that is 50%or less than that of France; (2) French residents own 50% or more; (3) Intragroup income is greater than 20%, or passive income and intra-group services income is greater than 50%	(1) German residents own 50% or more; (2) The foreign entity earns passive income; (3) Passive income is taxed at an effective rate less than 25%	N/A
Domestic shareholder ownership level necessary	10% or greater	10% or greater	Directly or indirectly hold 50% or greater	Any level of ownership	N/A
Foreign earnings subject to current taxation	Pro-rata share of passive earnings in most countries	Pro-rata share of passive earnings	Pro-rata share of all earnings	Pro-rata share of passive earnings	N/A
Additional features of CFC rules	CFCs resident in "listed" countries—those with similar tax systems to Australia—		CFC rules do not apply if the foreign subsidiary is located in another EU country and does	CFC rules do not apply if the foreign subsidiary exists	

	Australia	Canada	France	Germany	Netherlands
	have fewer types of income that may be attributed to domestic corporations		not exist solely to avoid French taxation	in another EU or European Economic Area country and conducts genuine economic activities	
Additional Anti-avoidance Rules	Foreign investment fund rules	Offshore investment fund rules	Abuse of law doctrine	General anti-avoidance rule	Low-taxed passive shareholding rules

Source: GAO analysis of country information.

Note: This table shows general treatments. It does not present all of the details, exceptions, or rules that govern the tax treatment of foreign-source income for our study countries.

[a] The percentage ownership by the domestic shareholder corresponds to the type of shares that were presented in table 2.

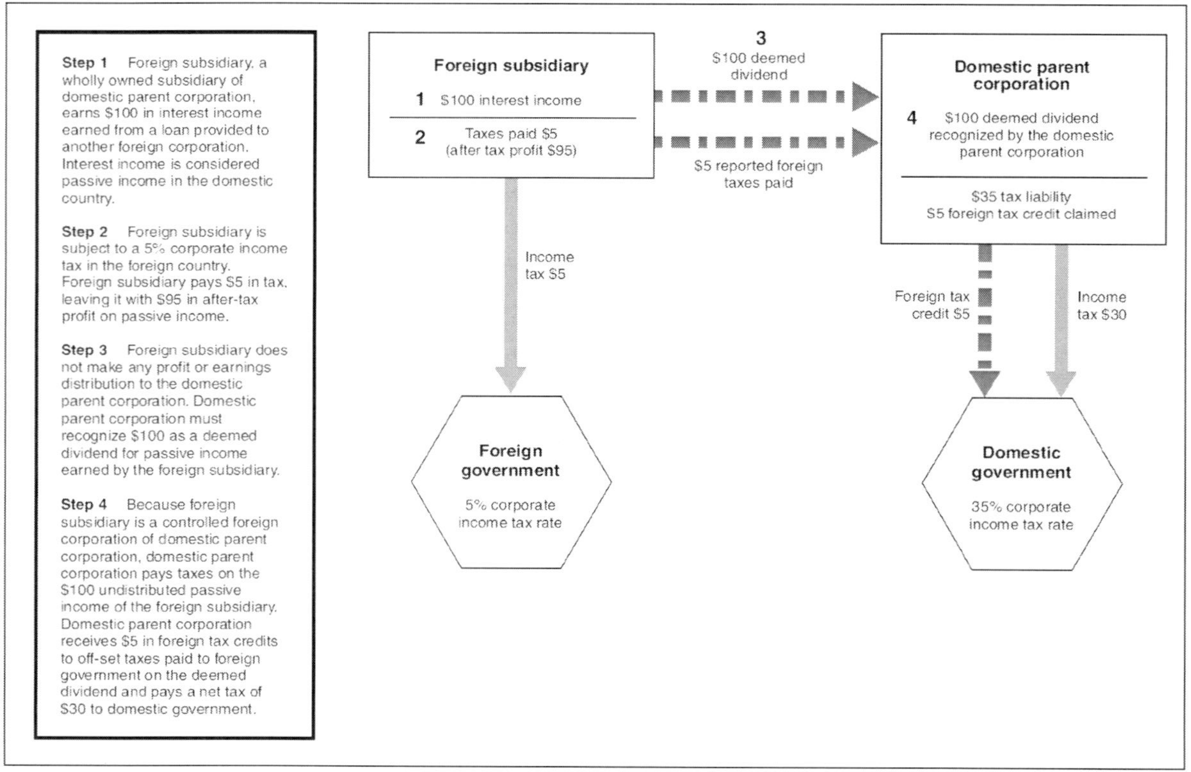

Source: GAO.

Figure 4. Simple Depiction of CFC Rules.

Study Countries Face Areas of Compliance Risk and Burden Known to Exist in the United States

Differences in tax rates across countries and differences in the taxation of different types of income may create incentives to avoid tax by shifting income from a high tax jurisdiction to a lower taxed jurisdiction or by converting income from a taxable type to tax-exempt type. Such efforts to reduce taxes may sometimes be legal tax avoidance, but may also be illegal noncompliance.

Tax experts identified four areas as sources of compliance risk or taxpayer compliance burden in our study countries. None of our study countries were able to provide quantitative estimates of the extent of noncompliance with their tax laws governing foreign-source income or the amount of compliance burden placed on taxpayers. Furthermore, an exhaustive list of all sources of compliance risk and burden does not exist. However, four areas that tax experts, including tax agency officials, tax practitioners, and academics identified were:

- transfer pricing,
- anti-avoidance rules,
- foreign tax credits, and
- domestic expense deductions.

These areas are also viewed by the Internal Revenue Service (IRS) or other tax experts as sources of compliance risk or compliance burden in the United States.

While countries establish rules in these four areas to serve a variety of policy goals, including maintaining economic competitiveness and avoiding double taxation, one important consideration is protecting the domestic tax base. One unique tax administration challenge that MNCs present is that they can shift income and assets among related entities in different countries to convert taxable income, either foreign or domestic, to tax-exempt or lower-taxed foreign-source income. The laws and regulations in these four areas are intended, in part, to protect the domestic tax base by preventing MNCs from mispricing transactions, relocating domestic passive income, misusing foreign tax credits, or reallocating expenses in ways that inappropriately reduce domestic taxes. These laws also create compliance burden, often requiring taxpayers to maintain detailed records and conduct complex analyses of international transactions.

Transfer Pricing, Particularly for Intangible Property, Is a Major Compliance Risk and Source of Compliance Burden in all of the Study Countries

Many tax agency officials we met with stated that transfer pricing was the most significant compliance risk they face in the area of international taxation. Similarly, many business representatives said complying with transfer pricing rules was often the most burdensome aspect of international taxation. Transfer prices are the prices of goods and services transferred among related entities within an MNC. These prices create compliance risks because MNCs can sometimes deliberately manipulate them to shift income from one related entity to another in order to reduce tax liability. For example, a parent corporation that charges a foreign subsidiary a below-market price for a good or service lowers the parent corporation's taxable income and raises the subsidiary's taxable income. Depending on tax rates and rules governing exemption and deferral, shifting income in this way may reduce an MNC's overall tax liability. An above-market price would shift taxable profits from the subsidiary to the parent.

Because transfer prices can shift taxable income from one country to another, all of our study countries have focused attention on transfer pricing with emphasis on stringent documentation requirements and audits. Generally, the study countries require taxpayers to provide evidence that transfer prices meet an arms-length standard, which means pricing transactions as if they occurred between unrelated parties. Establishing an arms-length price can be difficult when there is no comparable market price, such as for a unique good, service, or intangible property.

Although comprehensive data were not available, several experts, including the OECD, have noted that a significant amount of trade occurs between related parties.[15] Trade in services in the United States, while not a measure of overall U.S. trade, provides an example. According to the U.S. Bureau of Economic Analysis, trade in services between CFCs and related parties increased (in nominal dollars) from approximately $38.4 billion in 1999 to approximately $178.7 billion in 2006.[16]

The changing nature of international trade, particularly the growing trade in intangibles, is making international transactions more susceptible to transfer pricing abuse.[17] Tax experts repeatedly identified intangible property as a particular challenge when attempting to establish a transfer price that meets the arm's length standard. The unique nature of many intangible assets, such as patents, trademarks, copyrights, and brand recognition, means that it is difficult or impossible to identify comparable transactions for transfer pricing purposes. The revenue risk posed by mispricing intangibles can be significant because it can result in a company converting taxable income into tax-exempt or lower taxed income. For example, a parent corporation can license a patented computer technology to a foreign subsidiary and charge a below-market royalty, which is taxed in the domestic country. The subsidiary, which is in a low-tax country, uses the technology to generate a profit. The subsidiary then pays a tax-exempt dividend to the parent corporation. The parent corporation's country loses tax revenues because the tax-exempt dividend received is inflated and the taxable royalty is reduced. Conversely, the subsidiary's country receives additional tax revenues because the subsidiary's income is higher than it should be, as the smaller royalty payment is a deductible expense. In the aggregate, however, the MNC reduces its tax liability because the tax rate in the subsidiary's country is lower than the tax rate in the parent corporation's country.

Because identifying comparable prices for intangibles is often difficult, tax agencies and taxpayers often rely on a profit-split approach. The goal is to determine the percentage of profit attributable to buyers and sellers in different countries. Company officials consistently reported that making these determinations often requires costly special studies done by outside technical experts. In Australia, for example, to help protect against penalties, it is recommended that companies document that they followed a four-step process including selecting and justifying a transfer pricing methodology and then conducting an analysis based on that methodology to determine an arm's-length price. Appendix II provides details on the transfer pricing documentation and filing requirements for all of our study countries. One company official further said that even after making these investments, tax authorities may disagree with the results because of differences in opinion about the assumptions that had to be made. A number complained about transfer pricing reviews turning into disputes between countries over the distribution of tax liabilities. This can occur because, in many transfer pricing disputes, there are at least three interested parties, the taxpayers and two tax agencies. When a taxpayer reaches an agreement with one government on a price it can result in a lower tax payment for the other government.

On the other hand, tax agency officials repeatedly told us that they needed detailed information on the pricing methodologies used in order to verify that companies' prices satisfy the arm's-length standard. Tax agency officials said documentation of the data used and analysis conducted are critical to conducting independent determinations of the appropriateness of transfer prices. As one example of the importance tax agencies place on this documentation, the Australian Tax Office (ATO) has a system for rating the documentation quality. Under this system, poorly documented transfer pricing decisions are more systematically identified, allowing better targeting of audits.

Transfer pricing abuse is also known to be a significant problem in the United States. For example, IRS lists transfer pricing abuse as a high-risk compliance area because of the large number of taxpayers and significant dollar risk.

While there is agreement that transfer pricing is a major compliance risk in both our study countries and the United States, there is no consensus among the tax experts we met with about whether the compliance risks are greater in our study countries' exemption systems or in the United States' deferral system. Some argued that the tax benefits for an MNC from manipulating transfer prices are potentially larger under an exemption system than a deferral system. They argue that gains from transfer pricing abuse are larger if income can be made tax-exempt rather than tax-deferred. However, other experts pointed out that transfer pricing abuse is already a significant problem in the United States. Some of these experts noted that the incentives to avoid or evade tax under a deferral system can be quite large because tax can be deferred indefinitely. One of these experts also pointed out that there is no empirical evidence supporting the claim that countries with exemption systems face greater noncompliance with transfer pricing rules.

Study Countries Have Placed Greater Emphasis on Enforcing Transfer Pricing Rules

According to tax agency officials and outside tax experts, all study countries are placing greater emphasis on transfer pricing when auditing MNCs. For example, a tax practitioner in France said that the overwhelming majority of the audit issues he faces are transfer-pricing related. Another tax practitioner made the same observation about Germany, saying that there is a general perception that the burden for complying with transfer pricing has increased in recent years. These and other company representatives we spoke with said that time spent determining and documenting transfer prices in accordance with country requirements is a primary source of burden. These findings are echoed in the research of others. For example, according to a survey of 850 MNCs, 65 percent of respondents believe that transfer pricing documentation is more important now than it was 2 years ago.[18] Similarly, two-thirds of those respondents said they increased their resources on transfer pricing experts and studies in the last 3 years.

All Study Countries Use Advanced Pricing Agreements to Address Compliance Risks

All of the study countries have developed advanced pricing agreement (APA) programs that allow taxpayers and tax agencies to resolve transfer pricing issues before tax returns are filed and without the need for time consuming and expensive audits. Tax experts' opinions on APA participation varied, but often these experts did not consider them an efficient use of resources for addressing transfer pricing issues. Due to the time and resources required to obtain an APA, some taxpayers only pursue them for high-value transactions. Guidance provided by the Australian Tax Office illustrates the time and extensive documentation that can be required for an APA. The document, included in appendix III, lists requirements such as numerous meetings with agency officials, details of the transfer pricing methodology, and data supporting that methodology. The amount of time needed to complete an APA can be greater when it involves multiple countries. According to statistics from some of our study countries, APAs may take a year, or multiple years, to finalize. Between 1992 and the end of 2007, Canada finalized 153 APAs.

Some tax practitioners said that the decision to use APAs can also depend on the perceived risk that a transaction is likely to be subject to audit. Some taxpayers determine that APAs are less burdensome than going through an audit.

Complying with and Enforcing Anti-avoidance Rules, both CFC and Other Rules, Presents Challenges in All of Our Study Countries

According to taxpayers and tax officials we spoke with from the study countries, rules limiting the tax advantages of earning certain types of income offshore can serve as a source of taxpayer compliance burden and can be subject to compliance risk. As shown earlier in table 5, all of our study countries with the exception of the Netherlands use CFC rules as a primary method to limit the exemption or tax-deferral of certain income held offshore.[19] In addition, all of our study countries, including the Netherlands, have additional anti-avoidance rules that may apply and disallow tax advantages on specific types of income earned offshore. See appendix IV for details of other anti-avoidance rules in our study countries and in the United States. The study countries were not able to provide us with statistics on the number of subsidiaries subject to these anti- avoidance rules, the amount of income earned by them, or the residual tax revenue they generated.[20] Government officials we spoke with in several countries estimated the revenue generated from these rules to be low. However, some tax experts we spoke with stated that these rules played an important role in preventing MNCs from avoiding domestic taxes by earning income through CFCs.

When CFC rules are triggered, it can result in an increase in the MNC's tax liability. As a result, some of the tax practitioners we talked to said that structuring subsidiaries to avoid CFC rules requires careful planning and continuous monitoring. It is even possible that the actions of others could change a foreign subsidiary's CFC status. For example, as shown in table 5, one way a subsidiary of an Australian MNC can be a CFC is if five or fewer Australian investors own more than 50 percent of its shares. Consequently, a subsidiary that is not currently a CFC could become one if other Australian investors increase their ownership share.

Some tax practitioners told us that the complexity of the requirements for determining whether CFC rules applied and the amount of information needed to support a determination created considerable burden. For example, a French tax professional said that France's CFC rules are burdensome because they require the taxpayer to make a series of complex determinations (these were summarized in table 5)—such as whether the foreign tax liability of a subsidiary is greater or less than 50 percent of what it would be had the income been earned in France—in order to decide whether the subsidiary is a CFC. Given differences in accounting and tax rules between France and a foreign subsidiary's home country, these calculations can become complicated. German CFC rules require similar comparisons of actual taxes paid to theoretical taxes owed in determining whether the subsidiary will be taxed as a CFC. Australia takes a different approach, providing a list of countries where CFCs can be located and have fewer types of income that may be attributed to domestic corporations. It is not clear the extent to which this reduces burden in comparison to the other study countries.

Tax experts in Canada also said that acquiring information for documentation requirements related to CFC rules is particularly burdensome. For example, a Canadian firm with a 10 percent holding in a foreign subsidiary is required to provide the Canada Revenue Agency (CRA) with detailed tax and operations information from the foreign subsidiary. With only a 10 percent ownership stake, the Canadian firm may find it challenging to obtain such information in a timely manner, or at all.

Generally, CFC rules intend to limit an MNC's ability to shift income, especially passive income, to foreign jurisdictions to avoid or postpone domestic tax. Enforcing these rules could be difficult if the tax agency is not present in the foreign jurisdictions. For example, some officials in France and Canada said they may not be able to obtain and validate information needed to enforce these rules. One French official stated that it is difficult to see if a foreign subsidiary located in a low-tax jurisdiction thousands of miles away was an active business or being used to shelter income.

While the Netherlands does not have specific CFC rules, taxpayers and tax officials stated that the compliance burden associated with other anti-avoidance rules can be significant. According to tax professionals we spoke with, the Netherlands has low-taxed passive shareholding rules, another type of anti-avoidance rule. Overall, the tax practitioners and experts we spoke with agreed that the compliance burden related to anti-avoidance rules in the Netherlands could be significant.

Exemption of Foreign- Source Income Reduces the Need for Foreign Tax Credits, but They Can Still Serve as a Compliance Risk

The study countries all have FTC systems; however, according to both tax agency officials and tax practitioners FTCs play less of a role in these countries than in the United States because of the extent to which foreign-source income is exempt. For exempt income, taxpayers do not have to track and report foreign taxes paid. However, FTCs still exist as the study countries use them to avoid double taxation on foreign-source income that is not exempt, such as income subject to anti-avoidance rules. Most study countries were not able to supply data on the amount of FTCs that are claimed by domestic parent corporations in their countries. However, some tax experts said that the extent to which FTCs are generated varies by country, the type of industry in which the MNC conducts business, and the overall structure and location of the MNC's subsidiaries. For example, according to one German tax practitioner we spoke with, FTCs in that country tend to be generated mainly by businesses in the financial and insurance industries or where CFCs are involved.

As shown in table 6, the study countries vary in the rules they apply to FTCs. Many of these rules address the extent to which companies are allowed to accumulate FTCs and use them to offset other types of income. For example, Australia requires that all FTCs must be used in the taxable period in which they are recognized by the taxpayer on their tax filing. Any FTCs that a company has accumulated that are in excess of the amount of domestic tax actually paid on that income are lost. Canada, on the other hand, allows companies to carry excess FTCs back into the previous 3 years or forward up to 10 years. The United States allows companies to apply accumulated FTCs across different types of foreign-source incomes, across multiple countries, and over multiple years. For example, FTCs accumulated for foreign taxes paid on royalty income can be combined with FTCs accumulated on dividend income.

Some practitioners said there was some burden in tracking FTCs, but generally these rules were much less burdensome than complying with transfer pricing and anti-avoidance rules. One tax practitioner from Germany pointed out that in instances where MNCs have numerous subsidiaries subject to anti-avoidance rules it generally results in more instances where income is subject to tax in two countries, thus creating additional burden to identify and track FTCs.

Canada's Rules for Determining if Dividend Income Is Taxable, with FTCs Allowed, or Exempt Is a Compliance Challenge and Imposes Significant Taxpayer Burden

Tax agency officials, taxpayers, and tax experts agreed that Canada's rules for tracking foreign-source income and determining whether the income qualifies for tax exemption are complex and challenging for taxpayers and tax officials. As discussed earlier in this report, Canada's rules for determining whether or not dividend income received from foreign subsidiaries is exempt from domestic taxation include ownership requirements, location and business activities in a treaty country, and evaluating what type of earnings (e.g., capital gains, passive income, or active income) the subsidiary is distributing as a dividend. Canadian corporations receiving dividend income that does not qualify for exemption are taxed on that income, although FTCs may be applied to offset domestic tax. Canadian corporations are responsible for tracking all foreign earnings to ensure appropriate taxation once the income is received by the Canadian corporation. Taxpayers said these rules are burdensome, in part, because they require information only available from foreign subsidiaries, complex calculations and adjustments to income based on Canadian rules, and monitoring ownership changes for the foreign subsidiary. Tax agency officials said the rules are a compliance risk because of their complexity and difficulty of validating adherence.

The Generation of Inappropriate Foreign Tax Credits Was Identified as a Compliance Risk in Canada but the Risk Was Uncertain for the Other Study Countries

One area identified by tax officials as a source of compliance risk in Canada is the generation of abusive FTCs to offset overall tax liability. Often termed FTC generators, these activities, for example, allow taxpayers to take advantage of definitions of debt and equity in two countries by setting up a subsidiary for the purpose of holding assets and generating an income stream in such a way that the income stream is subject to foreign tax but also receives an offsetting deduction so that there is no net foreign tax. The taxpayer then tries to claim a domestic tax credit against this foreign tax paid while ignoring the offset.

Tax agency officials in Canada told us that FTC generators are considered a significant compliance risk in their country. CRA officials said they were currently auditing a number of domestic corporations to determine the extent to which Canadian companies are participating in these types of schemes. Because there is often no economic purpose to such a transaction, one company generally pays the other a fee for participating in the transaction. CRA officials said, so far, they have identified a substantial amount in avoided Canadian tax from 2001 to 2005.

Several experts we spoke to with knowledge of the other study countries said they did not think FTC generators were a significant issue in those countries. For example, a tax practitioner in Germany told us that since the majority of repatriated income to Germany is tax exempt FTCs are not produced in many instances. Similarly, Australian tax agency officials said that since Australian rules require FTCs to be used immediately in the year they are recognized, it reduces the ability to exploit the FTC generator scheme. However, some experts also pointed out that there is always a possibility that taxpayers could structure specific transactions to produce improper FTCs.

Table 6. Overview of Rules Governing FTCs in the Study Countries and the United States

			FTC carryover	
Country	**FTC allowed**	**Some limits on the use of FTCs**	**Back**	**Forward**
Australia	Yes	Domestic tax liability on the foreign-source income	None	None
Canada	Yes	Domestic tax liability on the foreign-source income by country	3 years	10 years
France	Yes[a]	Generally only allowed for withholding taxes paid to eligible tax treaty countries	None	None
Germany	Yes	Domestic tax liability on the foreign-source income by country	None	None
Netherlands	Yes	Domestic tax liability on the foreign-source income	None	None
United States	Yes	Domestic tax liability on the foreign-source income by broad category of income (general or passive)	1 year	10 years

Source: GAO analysis of country information.

Note: This table shows general treatments. It does not present all of the details, exceptions, or rules that govern the tax treatment of FTCs for our study countries.

[a] French domestic law, generally, does not allow FTCs; income subject to foreign tax and not exempt from French tax is taxable net of foreign tax paid. However, most French tax treaties provide for a tax credit that generally corresponds to withholding taxes on passive income.

FTC generators are also known to be a significant problem in the United States. For example, IRS lists them as a high-risk compliance area because of the large number of taxpayers and significant dollar risk that these types of schemes present.

Study Countries Differ in How They Limit Domestic Deductions for Expenses in Order to Prevent Erosion of the Domestic Tax Base

Using sometimes indirect methods, all study countries limit the domestic deductibility of some expenses associated with earning foreign-source income. Tax experts said that methods resulted in fewer compliance risks and burdens as compared to more direct methods. The deductibility of expenses incurred to earn foreign-source income is an issue because of the effect on revenue. If domestic deductibility is allowed under an exemption system, then MNCs are able to deduct expenses even though the resulting income is not subject to domestic tax.

France and Germany provide an example of an indirect approach to limiting expense deductions. As shown in table 2, they require corporations to add 5 percent of their gross tax-exempt dividends to their domestic taxable income (making dividends effectively 95 percent exempt) as an offset for deductible expenses incurred to earn the dividends. In our interviews with tax officials and members of the business community, this approach was cited as being less burdensome than tracing or allocating domestic expenses to tax-exempt income. Tracing would involve matching specific expenses to actual income generated. Some tax experts that we spoke to generally agreed that tracing would be ineffective. Many of the domestic expenses incurred by domestic corporations to invest or maintain an investment in a foreign subsidiary are general to the domestic corporation. These expenses include general management expenses, interest expense on borrowed money, and other administrative expenses. Because these expenses are general to the corporation, they are difficult to trace to the income items.

One alternative to tracing, mentioned by several experts we talked to, is allocating overhead expenses to income sources according to formulas. Rather than tracing expenses to actual income items, this alternative would allocate expenses according to a rule. Although not used in our study countries, allocating overhead expenses in this way could be made less burdensome than tracing. However, some experts stated that this approach would create compliance risks and burdens that do not currently exist. Several experts pointed to the United States as an example of this. In general, the United States requires U.S. corporations to allocate their expenses to a class of gross income and then, if a statutory provision requires, apportion deductions between the statutory grouping and the residual grouping. IRS officials stated that these rules were a compliance risk because corporations sometimes do not apply them appropriately. Some tax experts said these rules were a significant compliance burden because they are complex, requiring considerable time to conduct detailed calculations.

Another approach taken by all of our study countries is to limit the amount of interest expense that domestic corporations may deduct. Without limits on interest rates and amounts, corporations could shift income offshore and artificially increase domestic interest expenses, eroding the domestic tax base.

The rules vary by country and in many cases apply to all corporations, not just multinationals. For example, Germany and France require that interest rates be equivalent to arm's-length terms; the amount of expense that exceeds those terms is generally nondeductible.[21] Germany also has a rule disallowing interest expenses that exceed 30 percent of the corporation's adjusted earnings. Canada has a rule that targets interest paid to a foreign related-entity with a limit based on debt- to-equity ratios. With a few exceptions, tax professionals generally stated that the general types of interest expense rules described above did not pose much of a compliance burden.

The approaches taken by the study countries do not disallow all domestic deductions for expenses incurred with respect to foreign-source dividend income. However, some experts thought that the indirect approaches for limiting the deductibility of overhead expenses were more administrable and less burdensome than more targeted alternatives.

Australia, France, and Germany exempt active foreign-source income earned through foreign branches, but generally disallow domestic deductions for direct expenses attributable to earning the tax-exempt income. Direct expenses, like the cost of inventory, can be traced more easily to the income generated than more general expenses, like interest or other overhead costs.

Study Countries and the United States Do Not Regularly Report Basic Information about the Revenues Generated by Taxing Foreign-Source Corporate Income

In addition to lacking data about compliance and compliance burden for their foreign tax rules, our study countries lack data on the amount of tax revenues generated from the foreign activities of domestic corporations. This is also the case for the United States. Several federal agencies consistently report on the business activities of U.S. MNCs, but tax revenues are not included in these reports. For example, the Bureau of Economic Analysis reports on the foreign direct investment activities of U.S. MNCs and IRS reports data on the amount of income U.S. MNCs earn through CFCs.

U.S. international tax experts, including noted academics with multiple publications who we spoke to on this topic all agreed that regularly and consistently reporting U.S. tax revenue from foreign-source corporate income would be useful. They said that this information would help inform the debate about how to tax foreign-source income and potentially improve understanding of the role international tax rules play in the U.S. tax system.

For example, one of these experts pointed out that it was not widely understood how little domestic revenue is actually raised from taxing foreign-source income and that the tax regime governing foreign- source income plays a role in protecting the domestic tax base.

Treasury officials and the experts we talked to noted that producing regular revenue reports is feasible. A few academic papers and a recent release from the Secretary of the Treasury on international tax issues have reported estimates.[22] However, the experts said that these reports from different sources are not as useful as they could be because they are irregular, incomplete, and lack transparency. The experts felt that consistent and transparent reporting by a reputable government source that clearly describes the methodology used to produce the numbers and any limitations would be superior to the current occasional reports that sometimes lack much explanation. IRS and Treasury officials said IRS already collects the necessary data through corporate income tax returns to make the necessary calculations. Therefore, the tax experts said there should not be significant additional cost to the government to provide this information.

CONCLUSION

The United States, like our study countries, does not report the taxes collected by the United States on foreign-source income. Such basic information about the U.S. system would not be costly to provide and could contribute to the ongoing debate about the direction of U.S. policy. Such reporting would make explicit to policy makers, and perhaps to the general public as well, how little residual revenue is received by the United States from taxing foreign-source corporate income. Doing so could help highlight the important role that international corporate tax rules play in protecting the domestic tax base.

RECOMMENDATION FOR EXECUTIVE ACTION

We recommend that the Secretary of the Treasury use currently collected information to report annually on the revenue to the United States Treasury from taxing foreign-source corporate income. To enhance usefulness, such reports should describe the methodology and important limitations.

Agency Comments

We requested comments on a draft of this report from the Secretary of the Treasury. Treasury agreed with our recommendation. Treasury and IRS staff also provided technical comments, which we have incorporated as appropriate.

James R. White
Director, Tax Issues
Strategic Issues Team

Appendix I. Objectives, Scope, and Methodology

The objectives of this report were to (1) describe, for select case study countries that take a territorial approach, what types of foreign-source income the countries exempt and the rules governing those exemptions; and (2) describe, to the extent information is available, the compliance risks and taxpayer compliance burdens that the taxation of foreign-source corporate income presents for each of these countries.

To address our objectives, we selected five countries—Australia, Canada, France, Germany, and the Netherlands—to study based on several criteria, including range of tax treatments for foreign-source corporate income, unique tax system features, and Organization for Economic Cooperation and Development (OECD) membership. To gather information related to our selection criteria, we interviewed a number of corporate income tax experts, including academics, corporate tax practitioners, corporate taxpayers, officials at the OECD, and government officials. We contacted those experts that we identified through our literature review, which is described immediately below, along with experts that were recommended by other experts. Our literature review consisted of academic articles and books, national government publications, OECD and other multinational- organization publications on worldwide and territorial tax systems, and private sector research pertaining to various international aspects of corporate income tax systems and administration.

To describe the corporate income tax systems of our study countries, we consulted with corporate taxpayers, business representatives, government tax officials, and academic experts. We performed an in-depth literature review on each country's corporate income tax system, focusing on the rules governing international taxation. We also reviewed research-based publications produced by professional services organizations, academic experts, and international organizations. In general, we relied on information provided by tax officials from the study countries as well as published documents to summarize and characterize the corporate income tax systems for each country. We collected and analyzed data on the countries and their systems for taxing foreign-source corporate income, including tax policies, administrative mechanisms, compliance activities, and taxpayer reporting and documentation requirements. We did not conduct a formal legal review of the tax laws and rules in other countries, but relied on the information supplied by tax agency officials in those countries. We also provided the tax agency officials in our study countries a copy of our report to verify data and specific factual and legal statements about the tax laws in their country.

To address our second objective, we searched for publicly available data that quantified taxpayer compliance risk and burden for each of our study countries. In addition, we interviewed tax practitioners, taxpayers, government tax officials, business representatives, and officials from the OECD. We analyzed the information gathered through interviews as well as published documents to identify and describe the common sources of taxpayer compliance risk and compliance burden across the study countries. When available, we used publicly available data obtained from governments, private sector research, and academics to support evidence provided in the interviews. In addition, we provided tax agency officials from each of the study countries with a statement of facts that were presented in the report for their review and comment. Technical corrections were made to this report based upon country responses. This report shows general tax treatments and does not present all of the details, exceptions, or rules that govern the tax treatment of foreign-source income in our study countries and the United States.

We conducted our work from June 2008 to September 2009 in accordance with all sections of GAO's Quality Assurance Framework that are relevant to our objectives. The framework requires that we plan and perform the engagement to obtain sufficient and appropriate evidence to meet our stated objectives and to discuss any limitations in our work. We believe that the information and data obtained, and the analysis conducted, provide a reasonable basis for any findings and conclusions in this product.

Appendix II. Transfer Pricing Documentation Requirements in the Study Countries

Country	Documentation requirements	Time at which documentation should be prepared	Time to fulfill formal requests made during an audit
Australia	Documentation should evidence that the taxpayer has followed the following four-step process in setting and reviewing its transfer prices: **Step 1:** Accurately characterize the international dealings between the associated enterprises in the context of the taxpayer's business and document that characterization; **Step 2:** Select the most appropriate transfer pricing methods and document the choice; **Step 3:** Apply the most appropriate method, determine the arm's length outcome and document the process; and **Step 4:** Implement support processes. Install review process to ensure adjustment for material changes and document these processes.	Contemporaneous. However, generally only required to be submitted to the revenue authority following a specific notification, such as through an audit	28 days
Canada	Contemporaneous documentation required for cross border, related party transactions. Form T-106 required to be filed annually asks for reporting of non-arms-length transactions.	Must exist at the time of tax filing	3 months

Country	Documentation requirements	Time at which documentation should be prepared	Time to fulfill formal requests made during an audit
France	Taxpayers are not required to keep any transfer pricing documentation but are expected to cooperate with the tax agency in transfer pricing audits.	No formal contemporaneous documentation requirement.	60 days, but could be extended an additional 30 days
Germany	Documentation that shows the type and content of business transaction to related parties, including general information about (1) the group and ownership structure, (2) business relations to related parties, (3) analysis of functions and risks, and (4) transfer pricing analysis.	Contemporaneous for exceptional business transactions only	60 days
Netherlands	Documentation must show the arm's length nature of the transfer price that was applied.	Generally expected to be available at the time when the transaction occurs	4 weeks, but up to 3 months for certain complex transactions

Source: Organization for Economic Cooperation and Development and Ernst & Young.

Appendix III. Example from Australia of the Process for Obtaining an Advanced Pricing Agreement

Step 1: Pre-lodgment meetings

The purpose of pre-lodgment meetings is to:

- discuss the suitability of an APA
- allow a business to provide a broad outline of the proposed transfer pricing methodology
- discuss whether the APA will be unilateral or bilateral
- discuss the required documentation and analysis
- determine whether independent expert advice is required
- discuss Tax Office audit activity (if an APA is to flow on from audit)
- agree on a date for lodging a formal application
- agree on the APA timetable, and
- discuss the process for evaluating the application.

Pre-lodgment meetings do not bind either party to the APA program.

↓

Step 2: Lodgment of formal application

If proceeding with the APA, a business will be required to lodge a formal application.
The APA application should include:

- details of the proposed transfer pricing methodology, supported by relevant information
- terms and conditions governing the application of the transfer pricing methodology
- data showing that the transfer pricing methodology will produce arm's length results
- a discussion and analysis of the critical assumptions, and
- a suggested period of time for which the APA will apply.

For bilateral APAs we normally advise the treaty partner's tax authority once the application has been accepted.

↓

Step 3: Analysis/evaluation

We evaluate the data submitted and other relevant information, and seek additional information where necessary. We normally have numerous meetings with a business.

↓

Step 4: Negotiation and agreement

For a bilateral APA, the relevant tax administrations exchange position papers outlining the acceptability of the proposed transfer pricing methodology. A written confirmation of the concluded agreement is provided to the business.

For a unilateral APA, we provide written confirmation of the agreement we reach with the business.

↓

Step 5: Concluded APA

A concluded APA contains at least the following information:

- the transactions, agreements or arrangements covered by the APA
- the period and tax years covered by the APA
- the agreed transfer pricing methodology and the critical assumptions on which it is based
- the definition of key terms that form the basis of the methodology (for example, sales, operating profit)
- if applicable, a range of arm's length results, and
- the business's obligations as a result of the APA.

Source: Australian Tax Office.

APPENDIX IV. EXAMPLES OF OTHER ANTI-AVOIDANCE RULES IN THE STUDY COUNTRIES AND THE UNITED STATES

Table 7 provides some examples of non-controlled-foreign-corporation (CFC) anti-avoidance rules. This is not a complete list of the anti- avoidance rules in these countries. The consequences of falling under these rules are not necessarily the same as the CFC rules, but those consequences are beyond the scope of this table.

Table 7. Examples of Additional Anti-avoidance Rules by Country

Country	Regime	General definition of anti-avoidance rules
Australia	Foreign Investment Fund (FIF) rules	Certain Australian shareholders are subject to annual taxation on a deemed return on their pro rata shares of foreign investment funds if: (a) the foreign company or trust is not controlled by Australian residents; and (b) the taxpayer's shareholding is more than 10% of the total value of the taxpayer's interest in foreign companies and trusts; and (c) the foreign company or trust engages in "blacklisted" activities, such as certain financial intermediary, insurance, and banking transactions; and (d) the taxpayer holds the interest at the end of the taxable year.
Canada[a]	Offshore Investment Fund (OIF)	Canadian shareholders of an OIF are taxed currently on an imputed return basis where the investment in the OIF is established to be motivated by tax avoidance
France	Abuse of Law doctrine	General anti-avoidance law that permits the tax authorities to take action against legal arrangements or particular transactions when those arrangements and transactions were fictitious or undertaken for solely tax reasons.
Germany	General Anti-Avoidance Rule	General anti-avoidance rule, re-written in 2007, that prevents taxpayers from establishing legal forms or structures for the sole purpose of obtaining a tax advantage.

Table 7. (Continued)

Country	Regime	General definition of anti-avoidance rules
		Tax authorities may disregard structures for tax purposes in these situations.
Netherlands	Low-Taxed Passive (LTP) Shareholding	The Dutch shareholder that holds 25% or more, alone or together with an affiliate, of the shares in a (foreign) entity has to value its shareholding at market value in case the following conditions are met: (a) At least 90 percent of the assets of the subsidiary are, directly or indirectly, of a portfolio nature; (b) The foreign tax paid on profits is less than 10 percent of tax on profits if calculated under Dutch tax law; and (c) more than 50 percent of the carrying value of its property is not investment property.
United States	Passive Foreign Income Companies (PFIC)	A foreign corporation is a PFIC if: (a) 75 percent of the corporation's income is passive income; or (b) 50 percent of the corporation's assets (by value) are held for production of passive income. Unlike a CFC, a PFIC does not have any minimum stock ownership requirement. Each U.S. shareholder of a PFIC can choose to be taxed in one of two ways (or, in the case of marketable stock, one of three) ways.

Source: GAO analysis of country information.

[a] A more comprehensive 'foreign investment entity' (FIE) regime is proposed but not yet enacted. Under these proposed rules, Canadian investors in a FIE would be taxed currently on an imputed return basis, except where qualifying investors elect for accrual or mark-to-market treatment instead.

APPENDIX V. DESCRIPTION OF DIVIDEND EXEMPTION SYSTEMS IN JAPAN AND THE UNITED KINGDOM

Japan and the United Kingdom both adopted dividend exemption systems in 2009. These countries previously taxed dividends received from foreign subsidiaries but allowed for foreign tax credits (FTC) for foreign taxes paid.

Like our study countries, Japan and the United Kingdom have specific rules used to determine whether a dividend qualifies for exemption. Table 8 describes these rules.

Like the study countries, both Japan and the United Kingdom have anti-avoidance rules, including controlled foreign corporation (CFC) rules, which limit the tax advantages of earning or holding certain types of income in relatively low-tax jurisdictions. Japan revised their rules at the same time the dividend exemption system was implemented. The United Kingdom plans to address reforms to their CFC rules in future years. However, the United Kingdom did introduce a worldwide debt cap rule that limits the extent to which debt expenses can be deducted by corporations in the United Kingdom. One goal of this rule is to prevent situations in which businesses in the United Kingdom borrow excessively in order to invest internationally to produce exempt dividends. This is similar to some of the interest expense limitation rules we identified in the other study countries.

Table 8. Required Domestic Ownership Type and Level of Foreign Subsidiary to Qualify for Tax Exemption of Foreign-Source Dividend Income

	Japan	United Kingdom
Domestic ownership of foreign company	Direct shareholding of at least 25%[a]	Direct or indirect
Foreign company share type	Any type	Most types
Ownership duration	6 months	None

Source: GAO analysis of country information.

Note: This table shows general treatments. It does not present all of the details, exceptions, or rules that govern the tax treatment of foreign-source income in these countries.

[a] If the foreign company is a resident in a country with which Japan has concluded a tax treaty that provides for the allowance of an indirect FTC on qualifying dividends for a shareholding percentage of less than 25 percent, then the exemption can be applied in those cases.

End Notes

[1] These are U.S. corporations that claimed foreign tax credits on IRS tax forms. This may not include all U.S. corporations.

[2] Internal Revenue Service, *Corporate Foreign Tax Credit, 2003,* Statistics of Income Bulletin. Fall 2007.

[3] Under a worldwide approach, domestic corporations generally face the same total income tax liability regardless of whether an investment is located at home or abroad (assuming the foreign tax rate is the same or lower than the domestic rate), so investment location decisions are not distorted by the tax. However domestic corporations may not necessarily pay the same tax on a foreign investment as a foreign competitor. Under a territorial approach, domestic corporations earning foreign income only pay foreign tax, ensuring that they do not face a greater tax liability on that income than foreign competitors in the same country. However, this means that a domestic corporation could face different tax liabilities for foreign and domestic investments.

[4] See appendix V for additional details on the tax treatment of foreign-source income in Japan and the United Kingdom.

[5] In general, the U.S. tax system does not tax income until it is actually earned. The U.S. also generally imposes its corporate income tax at the corporate entity level. Deferral is a result of these basic features: anti-avoidance rules generally create exceptions to these principles in specific circumstances.

[6] For examples see Department of the Treasury, *Leveling the Playing Field: Curbing Tax Havens and Removing Tax Incentives for Shifting Jobs Overseas* (TG-119) (May 4, 2009); and President's Advisory Panel on Federal Tax Reform, *Simple, Fair, and Pro-Growth: Proposals to Fix America's Tax System* (Washington, D.C, November 2005).

[7] There is no standard definition of a subsidiary. For the purposes of our report, we use the term subsidiary loosely to refer to a chain of ownership whereby a parent corporation exercises a degree of control of another corporation. The level of ownership which determines control differs by individual circumstances. We discuss these scenarios later in the report.

[8] In general, branches of U.S. corporations are not regarded as separate legal entities for tax purposes.

[9] As shown in table 2, France and Germany effectively exempt 95 percent of capital gains from the sale of foreign subsidiary stock from domestic tax.

[10] As measured by the Canadian dollar value of total dividends received from foreign affiliates. Advisory Panel on Canada's System of International Taxation, *Enhancing Canada's International Tax Advantage* (December 2008).

[11] To qualify for the tax exemption, the French corporation must hold or intend to hold the shares for 2 years.

[12] Income taxed under anti-avoidance rules may, in some cases, be distributed to the domestic parent corporation as tax-exempt dividends.

[13] We use the term controlled foreign corporation (CFC) to describe foreign subsidiaries that are controlled by a domestic parent company as defined by each country. Some of our study countries use similar terms, such as controlled foreign company or controlled foreign affiliate, which we include in our use of the term controlled foreign corporation. Although this term has a specific technical meaning in several jurisdictions, including in the United States, we do not use this term in any of its technical senses, but as a generic description of these types of rules in various countries.

[14] In Canada, this income taxed currently is known as foreign accrual property income (FAPI). FAPI income includes categories of income that may not meet all definitions of passive income.

[15] OECD Observer, *Transfer Pricing: Keeping it at Arm's Length,* July 3, 2008.

[16] U.S Bureau of Economic Analysis. *U.S. International Services: Cross-Border Trade 1986-2007, and Services Supplied Through Affiliates, 1986*-2006.

[17] This is a significant issue for tax authorities because of the growing significance intangibles play in the global economy. Although there is currently no complete measure of the amount of income generated globally, or even in the United States, from investment in intangible assets, one indicator is the amount of income generated through royalty payments.

According to Treasury tax files, royalties paid by the top 7500 CFCs of U.S. parent corporations increased 68 percent ($22.4 to $37.6 billion) from 1996 to 2002.

[18] Ernst & Young, *Global Transfer Pricing Survey 2007-2008*. We did not validate the information reported in this study.

[19] As stated previously, we use the term CFC to generally describe foreign subsidiaries that are controlled by a domestic company as defined by each country. We do not use the term in any of its technical senses, but as a generic description of these types of rules in our study countries.

[20] Some of this data is available for U.S. MNCs based on corporate tax returns. For example, for tax year 2004, IRS reported the existence of 74,676 CFCs that earned $362.2 billion before income taxes. These CFCs paid $69.3 billion in income taxes worldwide.

[21] These requirements are related to transfer pricing rules in that they both aim to set the prices involved in certain related-party transactions at arm's length.

[22] Altshuler and Grubert reported U.S. corporations paid $12.7 billion in U.S. taxes on foreign-source corporate income reported in tax year 2000 in "Corporate Taxes in the World Economy: Reforming the Taxation of Cross-border Income" in *Fundamental Tax Reform: Issues, Choices, and Implications,* edited by John W. Diamond and George R. Zodrow (2008). The Department of the Treasury reported about $16 billion in revenue for tax year 2004 in *Leveling the Playing Field: Curbing Tax Havens and Removing Tax Incentives for Shifting Jobs Overseas* (TG-119) (May 4, 2009).

INDEX

D

E

F

G

H

I

J

K

L

M

N

O

P

Q

R

U

V

W

Y